HIS
CINDERELLA'S
ONE-NIGHT HEIR

HIS CINDERELLA'S ONE-NIGHT HEIR

LYNNE GRAHAM

MILLS & BOON

First published in Great Britain 2019
by Mills & Boon, an imprint of HarperCollins*Publishers*
1 London Bridge Street, London, SE1 9GF

Large Print edition 2020

© 2019 Lynne Graham

ISBN: 978-0-263-08400-9

MIX
Paper from
responsible sources
FSC™ C007454

This book is produced from independently certified
FSC™ paper to ensure responsible forest management. For
more information visit www.harpercollins.co.uk/green.

Printed and bound in Great Britain
by CPI Group (UK) Ltd, Croydon, CR0 4YY

CHAPTER ONE

DANTE LUCARELLI, BILLIONAIRE renewable energy entrepreneur, roared down the private road on the powerful motorbike, revelling in the wind against his skin, in the rare sense of freedom. For a very short space of time all his problems evaporated. And then that magical moment was over and he was recalling his duties as a guest and slowing down to enable his host, Steve, to overtake him.

'You let me win!' Steve growled, punching the taller male's arm in retribution as they parked the bikes. 'Where's the fun in that?'

'Didn't want to show you up in front of the locals,' Dante tossed back, his thick blue-black hair tousled, white teeth glinting in the sunlight against his lean bronzed features as he grinned down at his former schoolmate. 'Anyway, it's your bike... And so this is it? Your latest venture?' he added, glancing through the overhanging pine trees at the restaurant surrounded by decking and overlooking the swimming lake. Sited above the sandy beach, it had a funky, carefree, Caribbean vibe. 'Kind of small, isn't it, for a guy who builds sky-scrapers for a living?'

'Knock it off,' his friend urged, a burly blond man with the build of a rugby player. 'It's seasonal and does very well when the weather's good.'

'And employs a lot of those locals you like to take a paternal interest in,' Dante mocked, knowing Steve's sense of civic responsibility all too well. Steve Cranbrook was a kind man and one of the very few men Dante trusted.

They were in the south-east of France, a rural, far-from-touristic area where Steve had bought a chateau on a hill as a summer home for himself and his family. His all too numerous family, Dante reflected with a near shudder. Steve had four of the little blighters, two sets of twins under five, and they had been crawling over Dante and demanding attention ever since he had flown in earlier that day, which was why the break from the chateau was welcome. It wasn't that Dante disliked children, just that he wasn't used to them and weathering Steve's sociable kids was like trying to stand in the path of a hurricane armed with innumerable arms, legs and chattering tongues.

'It's not like that,' Steve protested. 'I just invest when I see the chance and contribute if there's a good cause. There aren't many employment opportunities around here.'

Dante took a seat at a wooden table hewn out of a giant tree trunk. Shrewd dark-as-pitch eyes swept the colourful bunting fluttering in the breeze as he picked up on the rampant beat of the music coming from the speakers and noted the youthful gathering at the bar. 'I bet this is the only party place in the neighbourhood,' he commented.

'Pretty much, but the food's good too. We get a lot of family trade when the beach is busy. So, tell me, when are you meeting with Eddie Shriner?'

Dante's lean, darkly handsome features tensed as the bite of his biggest problem sank its teeth into him afresh. 'In two weeks' time, and I still haven't got a woman on board to keep Krystal at bay.'

'I thought Liliana was stepping up as a favour,' Steve incised in surprise.

'No, that fell through. Liliana wanted an engagement ring as an inducement,' Dante admitted with an exasperated frown of recollection. 'Even though it would be a phoney engagement, I wasn't taking the risk of travelling down that road even with her.'

'An engagement ring?' Steve queried in surprise. 'Why on earth would she need a ring to pretend that she was your girlfriend again for Krystal's benefit?'

Dante shrugged a lean shoulder. 'She said it was a matter of pride, that she would lose face in front of Krystal if she didn't have a ring, because why else would she have reconciled with me when we broke up years ago?'

'Your love life…' Steve groaned, raking a rueful hand through his floppy blond hair. 'If you didn't dump so many women and leave them bitter and angry, you wouldn't be in this situation.'

Dante compressed his eloquent mouth in silent disagreement. He had no intention of ever marrying and producing children, and he had never lied to a woman on that score. He was upfront about his sex life and there was no room for love in it. Any woman who thought otherwise soon learned her mistake. He didn't get attached to women—never had, never would—and Liliana was the only exception to that rule. She was an ex who had become a friend and he genuinely respected and liked her, but he had still not been able to love her or want a more serious relationship with her.

Even trusting Liliana had initially been a challenge because Dante had never had quite the same view of women since he had caught his deceitful mother in bed with one of his father's closest friends. His snobbish mother, who stood in social judgement over others for their smallest mistakes and was quick to turn her back on them. He had soon realised that his parent regularly slept around. His indifference to Liliana had, however, told Dante all he needed to know about his own essentially cold heart. Without a doubt, he had inherited that ice gene from his unloving parents, he acknowledged grimly.

His sole experience of love had been his deep attachment to his older brother, Cristiano, and when Cristiano had died a year ago, it had shattered Dante and left him tormented with guilt. He often thought that had he been less selfish he might have saved his brother. Tragically, however, Cristiano had taken his own life because he had never been able to stand up for himself. Placed under intolerable pressure by their demanding parents and trying desperately hard to please as the eldest son and heir, Cristiano had crumbled and ultimately snapped under the strain.

And now the best that Dante could do in memory of his late brother was strive to buy back that little piece of woodland heaven where Cristiano had gone whenever life became too much for him. Sadly, in the wake of their firstborn's death, their parents had immediately sold that piece of land for the highest price possible to Eddie Shriner, a resort developer currently married to Dante's most embittered former lover. Even since marrying Eddie, Krystal had made several unashamed attempts to get Dante back into her bed. The woman was incorrigible and the last thing Dante needed was Krystal coming on to him while he was trying to make a business deal with her husband.

'You should hire an escort to play your girlfriend. *That* sort of a woman, someone you *pay*,' Steve disconcerted him by suggesting, his voice dropped to a discreet level across the table lest he be overheard.

'Sounds dodgy and dangerous,' Dante countered with a grimace, his attention stolen by the petite young woman standing by the bar with a tray.

Her hair was as multicoloured as a Halloween bonfire, a vivid curling mass of untidy copper, red and glinting gold anchored by a clasp to the back of her head. She had the porcelain pale skin of a true redhead and the legs and breasts of a goddess, Dante decided, following the slim shapely length of those fantastic legs down into the scuffed cowboy boots she wore teamed with a floaty short floral skirt and a fitted top, above which the swell of her lush breasts foamed like a desert mirage. Quirky fashion sense though, decidedly *not* his style.

'That's Belle. Er…ground control to Dante?' Steve joked when Dante failed to even look his way.

With difficulty, Dante dredged his attention back from those ripe, enthralling curves and the classic shape of the oval face above the display, and glanced wryly back at his companion.

'That's Belle,' Steve repeated with amusement glinting in his frank brown eyes.

'What's a looker like that doing waitressing in a place like this?' Dante demanded as he shifted restlessly on his bench seat, reacting to the all-male punch of pure lust pulsing at his groin.

'Possibly waiting for an opportunity like you to come knocking,' Steve mocked. 'Look, she's trying to save up enough money to get back to the UK and set herself up there again. You could step in like a good guy and fly her over to London with you.'

'Is this why you brought me here? Since when do I do anything for nothing?' Dante demanded, lifting his sunglasses to get a better look at that glorious oval face, only to discover on that closer inspection that it was unexpectedly dotted with freckles. He was almost relieved that there was a flaw in all that perfection. He wondered what colour her eyes were. Big eyes, *too* big?

'Of course not. It just occurred to me this minute that you could both do each other a favour. Why not *hire* Belle? She's in a jam… Oh, and there's a dog in the story too. You like dogs, no? Well, by all accounts she's a very *nice* girl, probably not your type at all. They've been running a book behind the bar all summer betting on which guy will make waves with her.'

'Charming,' Dante breathed, his nostrils flaring with disgust as he looked away. 'I don't do nice girls.'

'But this isn't one you would plan to *do*,' Steve pointed out very drily. 'You need a fake girlfriend, not a lover, and *she* needs the money. I offered her a loan but she wouldn't take it. She's got pride and she's honest. She told me she couldn't take the money because she didn't know how she would ever pay it back.'

'And she's a waitress. End of story,' Dante responded sardonically. 'I don't mess around with waitresses.'

'You're a snob and I never knew it,' Steve remarked in wonderment. 'Of course, I knew about the blue blood, the family *palazzo*, the title and all the rest of those trappings you claim to despise.'

'What would a waitress do if she was plunged into my world?' Dante enquired with biting derision.

'What you were paying her to do, which is more than you can say for most of the entitled women we both know,' Steve pointed out levelly. 'It would be a simple hire-and-fire situation but I'm not sure she would go for it. I hear she can be a bit of a hothead.'

Dante said nothing because he collided with the eyes of the woman coming to serve them. Yes, the eyes were big and they were a sparkling, unusually dark blue that verged on violet, very noticeable against that ivory freckled skin of hers.

While Belle was on her break she had watched the two men walk in from the car park. Everyone knew Steve, the British owner of the restaurant, a friendly and unassuming man in spite of his wealth and success as an award-winning architect with a string of international offices. Steve was also an unashamed family man with four beautiful kids and an even more beautiful Spanish wife, but his guest was as physically different from him as night was from day.

He was very tall, lean and powerful in build and he moved with the lithe precision of a man very much at home with his own body. His luxuriant wind-tousled black hair, falling almost long enough to touch his broad shoulders, blew back in the breeze, accentuating his hard, sculpted features. Even in jeans and an open-necked shirt, he was as sleekly magnificent as a black panther, physically beautiful in a wild, natural way and probably equally dangerous.

Several women peered out from the bar to admire his progress. Belle went back inside to do her job, silently listening as the bartender, a keen user of social media and a business student, identified the stranger as Dante Lucarelli. Evidently, he was some mega-rich Italian, a tycoon in the field of renewable energy. She walked over to serve Steve and his guest and as the Italian glanced up at her from beneath long black curling lashes that were wickedly wasted on a member of the male sex, she collided with vibrant dark golden eyes. For a terrifying split second, she froze as if a detonator had gone off inside her and her whole body burned as if he had set her on fire.

Flushed and filled with discomfiture, she took their drink orders and hastened back to the bar to fill them. She shouldn't have looked at him, shouldn't have looked anywhere near him, she scolded herself fiercely. He was extraordinarily good-looking and he knew it. Of course he did. Nobody saw a face like that in a mirror every day and failed to notice its lack of flaws and, even if he didn't look in mirrors much, every woman under sixty was studying him with appreciation and he could hardly be unaware of the amount of attention he attracted.

Belle's face was red and she hated that she couldn't stop that rush of self-conscious colour that turned her the colour of an over-ripe tomato. It embarrassed her as much at the age of twenty-two as it had when she had been at school and the butt of unkind jokes. Diminutive in height, red-haired, freckled, as well as overly endowed in the chest category, she had been very, very low on the cool scale of popularity at school.

Dante was hugely amused by the top-to-toe blush that had enveloped Belle. When had he last seen a woman blush? He could not remember, but then he didn't make the mistake of associating blushing with either shyness or innocence. He was much more inclined to link it to sexual attraction and awareness. He was accustomed to women looking at him and wanting him. After all, it had been happening since he was sixteen, when he had lost his virginity to one of his mother's friends, his rebellion after being confronted by his mother's extramarital fling. At the age of twenty-eight, he took it for granted that ninety-nine out of a hundred women would say yes to sharing his bed if he asked. And rarely did he even *have* to ask. Sex was frequently offered to Dante on a plate and without the smallest encouragement.

Belle delivered the drinks without once looking in Dante's direction and that overheated feeling in her body began mercifully to fade, allowing her to breathe again. It was normal to notice an attractive man, she soothed herself, and it wasn't her fault that she blushed fire-engine red. Just an unfortunate fact of life and she needed to learn to deal with it, as she had learned to deal with so many other unfortunate facts.

Predictably, her mind strayed back to the bad luck that seemed to thread through almost every wrong decision she made. She had been born to a woman who didn't want her, and a father who wanted nothing to do with her and told her so without embarrassment. Her grandmother, Sadie, had told her that that lack of interest was her parents' problem and not something that Belle should take personally. Her grandparents *had* loved her, she recalled with a prickling sensation behind her eyes, but her gran and grandad were both gone now and thinking about their loss only made Belle feel sad because it reminded her all over again that she was alone in the world with nobody and nothing to fall back on when things went wrong. And in France, things had gone very, *very* wrong for Belle.

Dante studied Belle as she moved round the bar, striving to imagine her dressed in haute couture, and that was a challenge when for some juvenile reason his brain only wanted to picture her naked. Clearly, a new wardrobe would make her infinitely more presentable but, of course, she would have to stop biting her nails. Such a disgusting habit, he reflected with distaste.

'What's she doing in France?' he asked Steve carelessly, angling his chin in Belle's direction.

'I only know local gossip. Word is she came out here about three years ago as a house-keeper/ companion for an elderly English widow living in the village. The widow's family hired her in London and left her to sink or swim as the old lady drifted into dementia. Eventually the local doctor got a little help for her but Belle was basically left to struggle.'

Dante slanted up an ebony brow. 'She sounds

like an idiot. Why didn't she just walk out and go home when the job got too much for her?'

Steve frowned. 'She was attached to the old lady by then and didn't want to let her down or abandon her.'

'How did she end up working here, in the bar?'

'The widow had a heart attack and died and as soon as the funeral was over, her family sold her house and left Belle homeless and without sufficient money to get home on. They also threw out the old lady's dog... Charlie,' Steve murmured as a small raggedy mutt badly in need of grooming nudged up against his leg for attention before moving on to eagerly greet another regular customer, who was more likely to offer him food.

Dante paid no heed to the dog, his attention resting on his friend. 'And then?'

'The guy who rents this place offered Belle an old campervan to live in. It's parked in the overflow car park behind the trees and she and the dog moved in. Then he gave her a job here.'

'So, she's pretty much one of life's losers,' Dante surmised without surprise. 'I'm more into winners.'

'But losers are undoubtedly easier and less demanding to negotiate with,' Steve remarked with cynical acceptance. 'And when have you ever been shy about profiting from other people's misfortunes?'

Dante grinned. 'Being ruthless is in my genes.'

'Except when it came to your brother. I lost count of the times you dragged Cristiano out of trouble,' Steve murmured, unimpressed. 'And you say you're not sentimental and yet look at the lengths you're willing to go to, simply to buy that woodland back.'

Dante's high cheekbones and strong jawline clenched hard. 'That's different.'

'It must be, particularly as I seem to remember that the first time you stayed in Cristiano's log cabin, you hated it like hell.'

'I don't enjoy roughing it, but Cristiano was always a back-to-nature freak,' Dante recalled abstractedly, his attention locking back on Belle as a couple of young guys flirted with her while she delivered their drinks. She wasn't blushing for their benefit, she was brisk and professional, he noted with helpless satisfaction. He signalled her with a graceful brown hand to order another set of drinks.

'Not for me,' Steve demurred with regret. 'Sancha will have dinner on and she hates it when I'm late for meals.'

'It's only nine,' Dante pointed out incredulously.

'Well, to be honest, my wife doesn't really like me out of her sight for too long,' Steve admitted with quiet pride.

Dante winced at the very idea of his freedom to do as he liked being curtailed in such a fashion.

'Listen, don't knock being married until you've tried it!' Steve protested in his own defence.

'I am never ever going to try it,' Dante assured him with a grim look of amusement. 'But I am in the market for a girlfriend I can employ and I may be late back tonight.'

Dante returned to watching Belle, his attention drawn involuntarily to the bountiful swell of her breasts as she bent down to lift drinks off the tray, not to mention the enticing curve of her bottom thrust out and the skirt rising to expose the backs of her slender bare thighs. He shifted in his seat again, his even white teeth gritting with irritation. He wasn't a horny teenager. Why was he reacting like one? She brought him his drink and he tossed a note down, telling her to keep the change.

'It's too much,' she said uncomfortably.

'Don't be silly,' Dante advised succinctly. 'I'd like a word with you in private when you finish your shift.'

'I'm tired. I'll be going straight to bed,' she told him swiftly. 'Sorry!'

'Don't blow me off before you hear what I have to say,' Dante urged. 'It's possible that I could have a job for you, a job that would eventually get you back to the UK.'

Belle tensed like a greyhound fired up at the starting line. Her eyes lifted from the table they had been carefully studying and surged up to his lean, darkly handsome features instead. There she clashed unwarily with stunning dark golden eyes and she took a very slight step back, gooseflesh tingling on her exposed skin. 'A job? What kind of a job?' she questioned.

A lazy grip on his beer bottle, Dante lounged back gracefully against the balustrade surrounding the decking. 'Later,' he murmured silkily. 'That is…if you can contrive to stay awake that long.'

Belle reddened at the comeback. He was so sure of himself he set her teeth on edge. He dangled the bait and then waited for her to jump. Well, she wasn't going to jump, was she? What sort of job could *he* possibly offer her? Aside from waitressing, her only work experience was in housekeeping and caring, and it was unlikely that he would seek to hire her for domestic work. Intelligence told her that a wealthy man would use an agency to fill such positions. On the other hand, she had no reason to suspect that he could be on the brink of offering her anything immoral. She was not irresistible, she was not the sort of bombshell that men moved mountains to impress or entrap, she acknowledged impatiently. No, the only sort of sleazy offers she got came from bored married men and randy young ones, thinking that a foreigner might offer a taste of something more exciting than a local. Though surely it wasn't beyond the bounds of possibility that Dante Lucarelli could have an elderly relative in need of care?

Then, even in that line, there were plenty of people with the paper qualifications for caring that Belle ironically lacked. Fate had forced her into a caring role after her widowed grandfather had become sick. She had had to drop out of school to look after him when he was diagnosed as terminally ill. But it would have been unthinkable for Belle to do any less when her grandparents had loved and cared for her since she was a baby.

Tracy, Belle's mother and her grandparents' only child, had been a fashion model in love with the high life, and when Belle's father had refused to marry Tracy after she fell pregnant, Tracy had refused to become a single parent struggling to survive. At only a few weeks old, Belle had been dumped with her grandparents. On the only occasion when Tracy *had* chosen to take Belle home with her, it had proved a disaster for both mother and daughter. Tracy was a man's woman and the man in her life always came first. That was why, in the end, Tracy had satisfied her maternal instincts by making regular payments to her parents in return for which they had raised Belle for her.

Between the ages of five and fifteen, Belle had not seen her mother once, merely following her parent's jet-set progress round the world with the aid of a map and infrequent postcards. It had been a huge source of disappointment and hurt to Belle when she was fourteen to be invited to live with Tracy and then just as swiftly be thrown back out of her mother's life again. Tracy's lover had made a pass at Belle and Tracy had caught him in the act. Although she had forgiven the man involved, she had not forgiven her daughter for the sin of having attracted his attention. After that episode, Belle had not laid eyes on her mother again until her grandfather's funeral, when Tracy had only come home for long enough to collect the proceeds of her parents' estate.

'For goodness' sake, you're old enough to be keeping yourself now!' Tracy had complained bitterly when Belle had asked her for financial help. 'Don't be looking for any more handouts from me! Your father stopped paying his dues for you years ago and now, *finally*, it's my turn to be free of you.'

Yet Belle had sacrificed three years of her life and the education she had badly wanted to nurse her grandfather. She had also conserved Tracy's inheritance by ensuring that her grandfather, Ernest, did not have to sell his home to fund his own place in a care home. Ignoring those unwelcome realities, Tracy had sold everything that could be sold and had left Belle penniless and sleeping on a friend's couch in London. Ironically, back then the advertised job in France with Mrs Devenish had looked like manna from heaven, Belle conceded ruefully.

Belle had needed somewhere to live, and London had been too expensive. In addition, the very idea of working abroad had seemed to promise adventure, something that Belle's life had sorely lacked. She had leapt in with both feet, believing that all she would have to do was cook, clean and shop and provide occasional companionship to a lonely elderly woman. She had assumed that she would have free time in which to explore and had never dreamt that she would end up trapped and working round the clock in a dull rural village without even a café.

As Belle helped to collect the last glasses, she glanced down at the beach, where she could see Dante Lucarelli poised below the pine trees. Was he waiting for her? *Of course* she was going to ask him about the job! She was not in a position to ignore even the vaguest chance of getting back home again because the restaurant would be closing for the season in another few weeks and then where would she be? She wasn't a French citizen and couldn't sign up for welfare or anything like that. At least in London, if she had no other choice, she could fall back on the benefits system.

Saying goodnight to the other wait staff and with Charlie faithfully following her, Belle trudged down to the beach. Dante was a dark silhouette below the trees and then he stepped into the moonlight, which made his black hair gleam blue and lit up his lean, strong features, highlighting his high cheekbones, classic nose and hard jawline. He needed a shave. A shadow of dark stubble accentuated his wide sensual mouth. With his eyes glittering colourlessly over her as he awaited her arrival in silence, Belle could feel herself getting hot again, as if her body was burning up inside her skin. Suddenly she was grateful for the darkness, knowing she was tomato red again.

'Belle?' Dante queried. 'What's it short for?'

'Tinkerbelle,' Belle admitted with extreme reluctance. 'Unfortunately, my mother thought that was a cute name for a baby girl but my grandparents called me Belle. Belle Forrester.'

'Tinkerbelle? That's out of a kid's movie, isn't it?' Dante breathed in surprise, studying her where she stood as stiff and still as though she were on the edge of dangerous quicksand. She had released her hair from the clasp and it foamed across her shoulders in an untamed curling mane.

'*Peter Pan.* Tinker Bell was the fairy, but *Belle* is a movie name too,' Belle told him with compressed lips.

'I guess if you'd had wings you'd have flown yourself back home,' Dante remarked very drily.

'So…er…the job?' Belle prompted tautly.

'The job would be a little unusual but completely above board,' he assured her and then, as though suddenly recollecting his manners, he moved closer to extend a lean hand. 'My name is Dante Lucarelli.'

'Yes.' Belle barely touched the tips of his fingers. 'The bartender identified you before you'd been seated for five minutes. He's a business student.'

'Tell me about yourself,' he urged.

'There's not a lot relevant to tell,' Belle retorted uncomfortably, wishing he would just get to the point instead of keeping her in ignorance. 'I'm twenty-two. I left school at sixteen with a bundle of GCSEs and I haven't had any educational input since then. I'd like to change that when I get back to London. These days you need training and qualifications to make a decent life.'

'If you know that why did you skip that opportunity until now?'

'I never *had* the opportunity,' Belle countered wryly, settling down on the concrete bench beneath the trees. 'My grandmother died and then my grandfather fell ill and needed looking after. After they were both gone, I took a job here, which was basically housekeeping but which turned into full-time caring as well.'

Dante lounged back against a tree trunk, all lithe, lean power and thrumming masculinity. He was as relaxed as she was tense. 'Is caring for older people what you want to do going forward?'

Belle stiffened. 'No, definitely not. I think professional caring's a job you need a vocation for and I don't have that.'

'Fair enough,' Dante murmured, increasingly surprised by her cool, unapologetic self-containment, because at the very least he had expected bubbly encouragement and flirtation from her. In his experience women came on to him whether they thought they had a chance with him or not, but Belle wasn't making the smallest effort in that direction. 'You may not have a vocation for the job I'm about to offer you either, but it *would* eventually get you back to the UK and I would *pay* you handsomely to do it.'

Belle twisted round to get a better view of him, wishing he would step out of the shadows so that she could see him better. 'Tell me about it…'

'I need a woman prepared to pretend that she's my live-in girlfriend. Faking the part would be *all* that was required from you,' Dante assured her with calm emphasis. 'The job would only last for a couple of weeks and then you would be free to pursue your own plans with the cash I give you. It would be a win-win proposition for both of us.'

Belle was rarely deprived of speech, but the shock of the nature of his job offer was sufficient to glue her tongue to the roof of her mouth because such an exotic possibility wouldn't have crossed her mind in her wildest dreams. 'But…er…you don't even know me,' she protested weakly when she could find her voice again.

'Why would I need to know you? Steve vouches for your trustworthiness. It's a job, a role if you want to call it that. It's casual and temporary but also financially rewarding,' he completed smoothly.

'But pretending to be someone's girlfriend would mean knowing stuff about each other, that sort of thing,' Belle protested in a rush. 'And we're complete strangers.'

'I'm sure a simple question and answer session would cover the basics you would need to know,' Dante fielded without hesitation. 'Think about this from my point of view.'

Belle's eyes widened. 'I don't know you well enough to do that.'

'Then let me do it for you,' Dante responded silkily. 'I'm offering you the job purely *because* you're a stranger and I will be paying you to provide what I require. As a stranger, you'll walk away afterwards without a problem. You won't cling or believe that I have any further obligation towards you, nor will you assume that having helped me out makes you special to me in any way.'

Belle stared back at him, stunned by that revealing little speech. 'Do women often cling to you?'

Dante tensed, glittering dark eyes locking to the pale troubled oval of her face. 'It's been a problem in the past. If there's a stage-five clinger out there, I've met her!'

'I'm not the clingy type,' Belle whispered abstractedly, marvelling at the impact of those compelling dark eyes of his even in low light.

'But you still haven't explained why you need a fake live-in girlfriend.'

'And I won't share any more of my private business unless you first express an interest in accepting the job,' Dante incised impatiently. 'Sleep on the idea. I'll see you tomorrow morning at eleven and you can give me an answer then. But be warned... I am a demanding employer with high standards. If you take the job, you'll have to meet all my requirements. That will mean wearing the clothes I buy for you, breaking the nail-biting habit... and ditching the dog. I'm not keen on dogs.'

Belle's shamefully bitten nails curled into her palms. He had *noticed*. She always prayed that people didn't notice her bad habit but it seemed horribly typical of Dante Lucarelli that he had noticed her stubby nails, and she was mortified. Almost at the same time she reached for Charlie for reassurance and lifted him up onto her lap, sand from his paws and coat flying in all directions. 'I can't possibly ditch Charlie.'

'He can go into kennels for the duration of our arrangement.'

'No, he needs love and attention, and taken away from everything familiar, he would be frightened!' Belle reasoned fiercely, hugging Charlie to her as if he were a worn soft toy.

'He's not a child,' Dante reasoned in exasperation.

'He's the only family I've got, and he's had a rough ride so far in life,' Belle argued in growing dismay. 'I won't part with Charlie!'

'Sleep on it,' Dante advised again. 'Now, let me walk you back to the campervan.'

'That's not necessary,' Belle told him, springing upright and setting the dog down. 'It's only a hundred yards away.'

'I decide what's necessary, not you,' Dante shot back at her, suspecting that she could be more trouble than she was worth because she was emotional, far too emotional. Cristiano had been full of emotion and very much prone to attachments as well and look where that caring, sharing nonsense had got his brother! Cristiano had left behind two heartbroken, seriously clingy and demanding chihuahuas and Dante kept them in exclusive boarding kennels in the very lap of luxury. He visited his brother's pets religiously once a month. It wasn't quite the same as taking the dogs home with him, but it was the best he felt able to offer dogs who had never been treated as dogs and who probably didn't even know that they *were* dogs. Tito and Carina expected to share beds, sleep on laps and be hand-fed from plates.

Belle breathed in deeply. 'Do you think maybe you're having to *hire* a girlfriend because you're so rude, heartless and authoritarian?'

'I can't remember when a woman last insulted me,' Dante confided in receipt of that refreshing question and gloriously untouched by the condemnation. A lifetime of criticism from his parents had ensured that he had developed a very tough hide.

'You must meet an awful lot of uncritical women.'

'Very rich men rarely meet with anything else,' Dante imparted with cynical conviction, pausing beside the small rusting campervan below the trees to marvel that anyone could actually be living in the battered vehicle full-time. 'I'll meet you in the bar tomorrow at eleven.'

CHAPTER TWO

IN THE CONFINEMENT of her bunk bed, Belle lay awake well into the early hours, pondering her choices, which only got fewer the more she thought about them. As always, she made lists. A long list of important questions that she *should* have asked but which Dante might not have answered. A list of pros and cons, again full of blanks, owing to her lack of facts on his situation.

'What do you think?' she asked Charlie ruefully as he cuddled up to her. 'We don't like or trust people who dislike dogs, do we? Do you think that's being too judgemental? Unfair? I mean, Steve's a lovely person and he's *friends* with Dante, which says something in his favour.'

Armed with her lists and clad in denim shorts and a light floral top, she walked up to the bar in the morning sunshine. The restaurant was being cleaned and it was time to prepare the tables for lunch. Hips twitching to the beat of the music playing, Belle set out place mats and glasses while she wondered if Dante was even capable of understanding how she felt about her dog.

Charlie hadn't started out as hers, but necessity had made him hers and they had been together since shortly after her arrival in France. She didn't have any family. She couldn't count the father she had only met once in her life or Tracy, who hadn't stayed in touch once her own parents were both gone. Charlie, silly and scruffy as he was, had become Belle's family. He wasn't the brightest of dogs, but he was always cheerful and loving and a wonderful comfort when the world seemed dark and she felt alone.

Dante, fresh from a late breakfast of kids and toddler tantrums, was in the mood to be charmed and the first thing he saw as he mounted the steps was Belle's bottom swaying in rhythmic time to the music. She had a gorgeous derrière, curvy and firm, and when she was dancing it was a work of art in the making, exactly what the average male wanted to see and take advantage of. Even so, he didn't *intend* to take advantage, Dante reminded himself doggedly, because as her potential employer, he would naturally be immune to her appeal. Sex didn't come into his dealings with employees. No matter how tempted he was, he would never ever make that mistake, he assured himself squarely.

'Sit down with me,' he told Belle as he strode past her.

'I can't. This is work time,' she pointed out, her gaze locking on him as though magnetised. 'I should've told you that last night.'

'I arranged it with your boss. You've got an hour off to be with me,' Dante informed her smoothly.

'But this is one of the busiest times of the day!' she exclaimed.

'I'm *paying* for your time off the clock,' Dante told her without hesitation.

Her face burned, hot as hellfire as she settled down at the table he had chosen. Money talked, she knew that, had long accepted it as an unpleasant fact of life. When people paid, they got to break the rules and call the shots. It turned normal into abnormal and deprived her of personal choice. She sat down opposite but her chin came up in challenge. 'I thought you'd come in earlier than this.'

'I slept in,' Dante declared without embarrassment. 'I travelled all day yesterday to get here.'

Belle was tempted to remark that he had undoubtedly travelled in luxury and could have no idea of the exhausting rigours of cheaper modes of travel, but she swallowed back the cheeky comment, accepting that she wasn't in a strong enough position to make it. She knew how to keep her lips sealed when she had to, knew all about serving in respectful silence regardless of how rude or provocative people were. That was one advantage of lowly labour, she acknowledged ruefully: it taught humility.

'I assume that you're considering taking

the job?' Dante lifted his level black brows in question as Belle's colleague delivered coffee to the table.

'Yes,' Belle confirmed, throwing sugar into the espresso because there was no milk available, and stirring it in haste. 'But you have to explain it first.'

Dante dragged in a deep breath and his T-shirt stretched taut as the strong muscles beneath the fine cotton flexed. Determined not to stare at his muscular chest, Belle looked at his face instead for the first time since they had sat down. Dazzling dark golden eyes gripped hers and her tummy lurched as if she had been plunged downward on a fairground ride. 'In two weeks' time I have a married couple coming to stay at my home for the weekend—Eddie and Krystal Shriner. I have a very important business deal that I hope to make with Eddie. The fly in the ointment is Krystal, whom I was fleetingly involved with four years ago. She's been trying to get back with me ever since,' he admitted stonily. 'And I don't want her flirting with me in front of her husband because that would destroy any hope I have of making a deal with him. He's a possessive man.'

Involuntarily, Belle's interest was caught. 'Is Krystal the stage-five clinger you mentioned last night?'

Dante nodded grim confirmation. 'Another woman living in my home with me would be a safeguard and the only possible precaution I can take. Your presence would infuriate her, but I will seem a much less attractive option if I appear to have already found a woman to settle down with. Krystal won't risk losing Eddie until she has a viable replacement in her sights.'

Belle grimaced at such calculation and settled back less tensely into her seat. 'Am I allowed to ask how long you were with this woman when you were involved with her?' she asked curiously.

His black brows pleated and his shapely mouth compressed into a flat hard line. 'One weekend…'

'One weekend?' Belle gasped in disbelief.

'And you've had all this trouble with her after that?'

'I didn't say she was normal,' Dante fielded drily.

'And they're going to be staying with you in London?'

'No, not in London,' Dante cut in. 'They'll be staying in my home in Italy.'

Belle was nonplussed. 'But I *thought* you were offering to take me back to London.'

'After the job's done my private jet will take you anywhere you want in the world, but we won't be travelling to London over the next couple of weeks,' Dante warned her. 'If you accept the job, I'll be taking you to Paris for new clothes. You can't possibly pass yourself off as my girlfriend with your current wardrobe. We will then fly to Italy, where you will familiarise yourself with my home and lifestyle. As soon as Eddie and Krystal have departed, the job will be over and you will be free to leave.'

Belle cringed at the prospect of Dante buying her clothes because that reminded her too much of her mother's financially lucrative and rather sordid relationships with men. Tracy was pretty much a professional mistress whose lovers paid for her expensive clothes, jewellery and cruises. Belle had been ashamed when she'd finally worked out the truth of how her mother afforded to live so well without ever apparently having to work and she was no longer surprised that her birth father had spoken with such derision about her mother, referring to her simply as 'the gold-digger'. Evidently even when she had been much younger Tracy had been busier bedding wealthy men than she had been modelling for a living. Belle was merely grateful that her grandparents had never grasped the truth about their daughter.

'So,' Belle said a little desperately as she trailed herself back out of those unpleasant memories and thoughts. 'The job as such would only last for a couple of weeks?'

'*Sì*... Yes,' Dante translated for her when she looked at him blankly.

Digging hurriedly into her pocket, Belle ex-tracted the lists she'd drawn up the night before. 'I have some other questions for you, if that's all right.'

'I suppose it has to be,' Dante conceded, watching her tiny tongue slide out to moisten her full lower lip with a fascination the exercise should not have commanded. Instantly he was imagining that tongue working a spell on his all too ready body and he gritted his teeth hard, furious with his failing self-discipline. He was spoilt when it came to women, he acknowledged, because it was rare for him to meet a woman he wanted that he couldn't have. But she would be working for him. He would be *paying* her. Adding sex to that arrangement would make it dubious in the extreme.

Belle painstakingly read her first question. '"Why do you not have a female friend willing to do this for you?"'

'I did. She changed her mind and decided it was a matter of pride that she have an engagement ring on her finger before facing Krystal.

I wasn't prepared to take the pretence that far,' Dante admitted flatly.

'My goodness, you're so much in demand with the women in your life, you must feel positively *hunted*!' Belle trilled back as sweet as sugar.

Dante played safe by taking the comment at face value and shrugged a broad shoulder in dismissal. 'Next question?'

'Charlie's a big deal.'

Dante frowned. 'Charlie? Who's Charlie?'

Belle bridled. 'My dog. You met him last night.'

'He's a dog, not a person. I didn't *meet* him,' Dante told her drily. 'The kennels I mentioned are not far from my home and I can assure you that they offer the very best of care because they've been looking after my late brother's two dogs for me for over a year.'

Belle studied him, aghast. 'You've left your brother's dogs in kennels for over a year?' she gasped in horror. 'Why haven't you brought them home with you?'

'I'm not a dog-oriented person,' Dante reminded her impatiently. 'Look, I can't even believe we're having this stupid conversation about animals. If you must bring the dog, bring it, but it will be sent ahead of us to Italy. It's not coming to Paris with us!'

Belle decided to quit while she was ahead. The arrangement wasn't perfect, but she could see that he thought he was being very generous with that concession and she didn't want to be so demanding that she talked herself out of the job.

'You still haven't said what you're prepared to pay me,' Belle remarked uncomfortably.

'What did you earn working last year?' Dante shot back at her, annoyed that he was going to have to live with a dog under his feet, no matter how briefly. She was an odd little creature, he decided, and far too attached to the dog, but such human quirks and his apparent acceptance of them could well make her seem more convincing in the role he was giving her.

Taken aback by that blunt demand, Belle

blinked and told him before she could think better of such honesty.

'Seriously…that's *all*?' Dante checked in apparent disbelief.

Belle reddened. 'That's all but it *was* a live-in position and those always pay less.'

'Multiply that sum by fifty and that's what you'll walk away with in a few weeks' time,' Dante assured her without skipping a beat.

'By *fifty*? You can't pay me that much and buy me clothes into the bargain!' Belle objected in amazement. 'That's an outrageous sum.'

'Deal with it. It's not an outrageous sum to me,' Dante declared. 'And if you make a genuine effort to meet the demands of the role, I'll give you a bonus as well.'

Belle was almost white with shock at the thought of so much money coming her way. Even frantic on-the-spot calculations screamed that that much cash would turn her life around and give her options for the first time ever. She would be able to come up with the deposit to rent a flat in London and organise some sort of educational course to make herself more employable. In fact, the sky would be the limit with a financial nest egg that decent behind her. She was ashamed of the truth, that his offer had made her mentally tear up her pros and cons list because a risk that would improve her life so radically seemed well worth taking. It was not as though she had anything to lose aside from Charlie.

'It'll be like winning the lottery,' she whispered helplessly.

'No, *I'm* the lottery you have apparently won,' Dante contradicted. 'Start getting into *that* role. What I'm willing to pay you will merely be pocket change when compared to the life you would lead living with me.'

'The pocket change wins though,' Belle told him. 'I think living with you will be a real challenge.'

Dante ignored that comment, rising above the temptation to inform her that having *any* woman living below his roof and invading his cherished privacy would be a punishment for him. 'I'll have travelling arrangements made for the dog and I'll pick you up tomorrow.'

'Tomorrow?' she echoed, blinking in surprise. 'That soon?'

'We haven't got time to waste and you can't have much to pack. Give me your phone number,' Dante instructed. 'I'll text you to let you know when we're leaving.'

As Dante cleared the steps down into the car park in a couple of strides to head back to his motorbike, Belle was left in a total daze. She went back to setting tables because she couldn't quite accept that she was leaving the restaurant and that her life could change so suddenly. On the score of packing, Dante had hit the nail on the head because she had very few possessions and an even smaller collection of clothing, she conceded. Though she would give Charlie a bath and a good brush to ensure that he looked his smartest and that he wasn't mistaken for some unloved and neglected stray. She would also have to thoroughly clean the campervan and pass the key back to her boss.

* * *

When Dante arrived to collect Belle the following morning she was in floods of tears over parting with the dog and the pet transporters his PA had organised were hovering beside their van, reluctant to step in and hurry matters along. Fortunately, Dante had no such inhibitions.

'Say goodbye to the dog, Belle,' Dante told her. 'It's only for a few days.'

'He's scared,' Belle whispered shakily. 'He's never been in a cage before.'

'Put him in the cage. How are you planning to get him into the UK?' Dante enquired. 'Presumably at some point of the journey he will have to tolerate a cage. This will be good practice for him.'

Charlie went into the cage and cowered at the back of it like a dog expecting to be beaten. Stifling a sob, Belle handed over the paperwork Charlie had arrived in France with two years earlier. 'He looks so pathetic,' she muttered wretchedly.

'Yes, he's feeling very sorry for himself,'

Dante agreed, thinking that Charlie should be onstage because he certainly knew how to work an audience. 'But you'll be reunited very soon. Pull yourself together.'

Belatedly, Belle registered that Dante looked very different. No longer casually clad in jeans, he sported an exquisitely tailored dark grey business suit that showcased his tall broad, narrow-hipped physique to perfection. Staring for a moment longer than she was comfortable with, she hurriedly twisted her head away. 'I am perfectly together. I was just upset,' she proclaimed defensively.

'Crying in public is not acceptable unless you're attending a funeral or a wedding. Saying goodbye momentarily to a dog is not a good enough excuse,' Dante informed her as her single bag was dropped in the capacious boot of the car and the driver yanked open the passenger door for them.

'S-sorry,' Belle said in a wobbly voice, turning her tear-stained face away from him as she climbed into the opulent car.

The car ferried them at speed to Toulouse-

Blagnac Airport, where they were rushed through the VIP channel at speed to board Dante's private jet. Eyes wide from her first glimpse of the opulent oyster-coloured leather seating and the sumptuous interior, Belle accepted the pile of high-fashion magazines the stewardess brought to her and tried not to stare while the same woman flirted madly with Dante with loads of hair flicking, smiles and a provocative wriggle in her too-tight pencil skirt that would've caught the attention of a dead man. Dante, however, remained remarkably untouched by the display and flipped open a laptop to work. Belle wondered if women always vied for his attention so blatantly and then asked herself why she was even interested.

He was a breathtakingly handsome guy, rich and sophisticated, as alien to her as snow in the summer heat. Her hormones went all out of kilter around him and she felt uncomfortable in her own body as it betrayed her in ways she hadn't expected. It had never occurred to her before that she could be attracted to someone she didn't like, that a mere flashing glance from tigerish dark golden eyes could make her breasts swell and her nipples tighten and a hot dull ache blossom at the junction of her thighs. That weakness was a revelation because it was new to her, but it wasn't something that particularly worried her.

She was convinced that she would never give way to that kind of temptation because she was painfully aware that sex meant very little unless it was accompanied by genuine feelings. None of her mother's many affairs had lasted or cured Tracy's essential dissatisfaction with her life. And Belle wanted much more for herself than a fleeting sexual thrill or a luxurious lifestyle. She wanted love, a man who would make her feel whole and safe, and when she finally found him, she would have a family with him, recreating the family she had both lost and never really had, she thought fondly. He wouldn't be a commitment-phobe like Dante, who saw women as clingy and probably didn't like children much more than he liked dogs. He would be an ordinary guy, willing to settle down when he met someone who made him happy.

'Have you ever been to Paris before?' Dante asked, watching Belle peer out of the limo windows like a child on a school trip, afraid of missing out on a single sight.

'No.'

'And yet you've been in France for…how long?'

'Almost three years.'

'Why didn't you travel around?'

'I couldn't leave Mrs Devenish or Charlie to look after themselves and, to be honest, I never really had enough money to go off exploring.'

'Then why did you lumber yourself with a dog into the bargain?' Dante enquired drily.

'He wasn't mine initially. Mrs Devenish's niece brought Charlie out here as a gift for her. Unfortunately, she wasn't well enough to look after a puppy, but she did enjoy seeing him round the house,' Belle confided ruefully. 'She was a lovely old lady but her relatives didn't want to accept that she was ill. They liked coming out here in the summer for their holidays and they insisted that I was exaggerating her condition. It took the doctor to convince them otherwise and by that stage, as it turned out, she only had a few more weeks to live.'

'You need to learn how to stand up for yourself more effectively,' Dante censured.

Belle shrugged. 'Only if you can afford to take the consequences and I had neither another job to go to nor anywhere else to live.'

'You shouldn't have put yourself in that position.'

'Haven't I just done the same thing again with you?'

Dante frowned at her in bemusement. 'What are you talking about?'

'Well, I don't have an employment contract or any safeguards with you either...*and* you've now got Charlie to hold over me,' she pointed out, lifting her chin.

'You can't think I'm likely to hold Charlie hostage? Or ditch you in Paris without money?' Dante breathed in a raw undertone, insulted beyond belief by her suspicions.

'Isn't that what I'm saying?' Belle murmured gently. 'Beggars can't be choosers. I've *had* to take the risk of trusting you.'

Dante released his breath in a pent-up hiss of displeasure and said nothing, his lean dark face grim. He didn't enjoy being taxed with the truth.

Belle stepped out of the limousine onto one of the most exclusive streets in Paris and stared wide-eyed at the even more exclusive hotel that Dante was striding towards. Her strained face flushed, and she smoothed down her floral skirt and studied her scuffed boots with embarrassment. She followed him into the foyer, careful to stay behind him and out of sight, almost skidding on the highly polished floor tiles and horribly conscious of the plush silence and the dulled murmur of well-bred voices. She looked up above the atrium entrance to the serried ranks of colonnaded floors above. Never had she been so aware of her shabby appearance and at any moment, if she wasn't careful enough and drew the wrong person's attention, she expected a hand to fall on her shoulder and someone to ask her what she was doing there, because she felt like an intruder.

'You've got very quiet,' Dante remarked as she shot into the lift on his heels and immersed herself in a corner. 'You have a busy schedule this afternoon.'

Belle looked up at him in bewilderment. 'Doing what?'

'Visiting the spa for beauty treatments. Don't ask me what's included,' Dante advised. 'I told my PA you needed a makeover, especially in the defective nail department. I'm afraid that perfect grooming goes with the territory.'

'I'm afraid you're stuck with my defective nails,' Belle countered snidely. 'There's nothing anyone can do with them.'

'Belle...if I was willing to pay the surcharge,' Dante murmured silkily, 'they'd cut off your hands and give you new ones!'

Belle paled and linked her hands together tightly, wanting to nibble nervously but afraid of the reaction she might ignite if she succumbed to temptation. The lift doors whirred silently back and a man in a white jacket began to bow and scrape.

'Our butler. Anything you want or need, you ask him,' Dante informed her, walking out into the vast space awaiting them.

Dumbstruck, Belle wandered across the floor and straight out onto the balcony to lean against the elaborate wrought-iron balustrade and stare in awe at the superlative view of the slender silhouette of the Eiffel Tower, the glass roofs of the Grand Palais and the bell tower of Notre Dame Cathedral.

'Madam…?'

She swivelled to register that the butler held a silver tray and was offering her a glass of champagne. She swallowed hard, only just re-sisting an urge to pinch herself to see if she was dreaming and grasped the champagne. Her glass in her hand, she was ushered back inside and up the swirling staircase to her bed-room, which was the last word in over-the-top glamour, from its brocaded walls to its soft and inviting velvet seating and subtle eau-de-Nil colouring. Far above her, ornate lace mouldings decorated the ceiling. She hastened into the bathroom and was disappointed to discover that it contained only a shower, although it was a vast wet-room affair that could have coped with a party and took up a good half of the room.

When she came downstairs again, lunch was being served and a young woman in a very stylish suit was using a tablet at Dante's elbow. 'Belle...this is my executive PA, Caterina. She will be scheduling your appointments here because I have meetings to attend.'

Belle sat down opposite Dante to have lunch. Not having eaten since breakfast, she was starving. Dante and his PA talked in Italian while she ate, and she watched Dante's eyes shimmer pure gold in the sunlight before his ridiculously long black lashes skimmed down to shade them. Her mouth ran dry, her throat tightening, sudden nerves assailing her. Her fingers lifted to her mouth and at the exact same moment, Dante flashed a warning look at her. 'Try it and I'll plunge your hands into bowls of ice water!' he threatened impatiently.

Her colour rising, Belle dropped her hand back to her lap. 'Stop threatening me!' she snapped back at him.

'You have to learn sometime,' Dante told her while Caterina watched the byplay in seeming fascination. 'I'll take you out to dine somewhere tonight…' He turned back to his PA. 'Make sure she's camera-ready.'

'Why would I need to be camera-ready?' Belle demanded.

'Because I expect that we will be papped at some stage of the evening.'

'Papped?'

'The paparazzi,' Caterina explained. 'Dante's social life is always hot news in Italy.'

Caterina escorted her downstairs to the spa facilities. Belle endured one treatment after another, finally relaxing into the procedures when the less pleasant experiences were behind her. She flexed her fake nails, now long and shaped and a pale, barely noticeable pink. She reckoned not a single hair now existed anywhere on her body aside from her brows and her head. The facial and the massage that followed were soothing and the treatments concluded with an appointment with a hair stylist, who lamented at length over the sun damage to her bountiful tresses and then quietly and efficiently transformed her unmanageable mane into a sleek fall as smooth and straight as silk.

Back in her bedroom she was greeted by three women with mobile racks of clothing and cases of other items. Her size established, she didn't get away with being shy. She donned elaborate silky lingerie while the most senior woman muttered about a good foundation for clothing being very important to an elegant appearance. Then she had to model outfit after outfit while the women argued amongst themselves about which colours and designs best suited her. She had never seen such beautiful, expensive material before or garments put together with so exceptional a finish and fit. But considering that Dante only required her to play his girlfriend for one weekend, she couldn't credit the sheer size and diversity of the wardrobe that he evidently deemed necessary. She recalled that she would have to live her role in his home for a few days beforehand but still rolled her eyes at his extravagance. Only when she saw her unfamiliar reflection in a mirror did she stop rolling her eyes and stop worrying about what he had chosen to spend.

There she was garbed in a very slightly sparkly blue dress that might have been specially designed for her, shoestring straps adorning her shoulders, a superbly designed backless bra restraining her exuberant breasts, the hemline swirling well above her knees, her feet shod in perilously high sandals. She looked taller, slimmer, less overwhelmingly busty and she breathed a little easier, grabbing up the clutch that toned with the shoes to go down the stairs.

'Very classy...' Dante pronounced approvingly, watching her descent from below, and yet there was the strangest kernel of disappointment at the heart of his reaction. He realised in surprise that on some level he had liked the untamed curls, the youthful eccentric clothes, and that truth shook him. Indisputably, Belle looked more gorgeous than the first time he had seen her but somehow, inexplicably, she had been hotter and sexier in her own natural style.

'You're getting what you paid for,' Belle fielded with an awkward shrug.

His dark deep-set eyes flared with golden highlights. 'Don't dwell on that aspect. It's not important.'

Dante studied her long shapely legs and imagined lifting the skirt and running his hands up those slim, smooth thighs. A very faint shudder ran through him as he stamped down hard on that lusty image and attempted to quell the heat at his groin while reminding himself that he wasn't going to go there, wasn't going to yield to that kind of dangerous impulse. Of course, he would have to touch her. In the roles they were playing, a certain amount of physical contact was unavoidable, but he would ensure that it was only enough to give a superficial if convincing impression.

In the lift, the lustrous glow of Dante's stunning eyes sent tiny little tremors travelling up through Belle's legs. She felt weak, dizzy, and the lift felt claustrophobic. At the very heart of her she could feel a pulse pounding out her tension like a drum while her breasts ached beneath her clothing. Attraction, just stupid body chemistry, she told herself dismissively as she climbed into the back of the glossy limousine awaiting them.

The silence hummed as she gazed back at him, every nerve ending in her body tight with tension. His eyes were brilliant gold, striking, utterly compelling and she swallowed hard. Dante succumbed to a 'what the hell?' prompt, because he had never been into self-denial. How the blazes could they hope to pretend to be lovers if he had yet to even touch her? he asked himself. That was nonsense. That decision forged, he reached out a hand and she clasped it, allowing him to propel her across the seat into his arms. She went without even having to think about it, her heart pounding so fast she felt light-headed.

His big hands framing her face, he kissed her with so much hunger she was blown away by the experience. Her heart raced even faster, her body tense and throbbing on the edge of an anticipation she had never felt before. Her tense fingers clenched into the collar of his jacket. He crushed her lips with a groan and his tongue stole between them, delving deep for a skilful exploration that acted like a wake-up call for every fibre of her being. Nobody had ever made her feel what he was making her feel and it was wildly unexpected and unbelievably exciting, and the experience engulfed her like an avalanche. She was in over her head before she knew it.

'Bad timing, *amante*,' Dante growled, his hips arching up slightly as she braced a steadying hand on a lean masculine thigh, dangerously close to the tented fabric doing a very poor job of concealing his excitement. For the first time in his life he *wanted* a woman to be bold and he waited for a split second; however, frustratingly, she made no move. 'I can tell the driver to drive us around...'

That suggestion spooked Belle. She moistened her swollen lower lip, her attention locked to his reddened mouth, her entire being, it seemed, caught up in the need for him to touch her again and satisfy the surge of need that had come out of nowhere to make her tremble and perspire. 'Er…'

'*Madonna mia… Ti voglio…* I want you,' Dante framed raggedly, claiming her ripe lips with his again at the same time as he pressed her hand to the part of him that most craved her attention.

Her fingers spread across the fabric, hesitantly tracing the long thick length of him through the fine fabric of his trousers, and that suddenly she was into frighteningly unfamiliar territory because she never ever played the tease, never encouraged where she had no plans to deliver, but just then she was dealing with a level of temptation new to her. No man had ever got her to the point where she wanted more than a kiss or even to the point where she truly wanted *him*. In a matter of minutes, Dante had accomplished both feats and shocked her witless because in his arms she was learning that even logical thought was more of a challenge than she could manage.

Her startled eyes flew up to his smouldering appraisal and she burned inside and out, her temperature climbing in direct response to the predatory hunger she saw in him and that on some level she actually craved. 'I thought we were going to eat,' she reminded him shakily, striving with a sense of cowardice to escape a situation that she knew she had helped to create because she hadn't said no and she hadn't pushed him away.

'I can feed you back at the hotel,' Dante husked, catching her hand in his as she backed away from him to prevent her retreat.

'Sex isn't part of our arrangement…is it?' Belle demanded in sudden dismay.

'Of course not,' Dante assured her silkily, smoothing her small fingers in his to keep her close. 'But what we choose to do outside those boundaries is our business alone.'

'Er, well…yes, but I don't think we should

be getting *too* friendly,' Belle mumbled in an awkward rush, trailing her hand free of his.

'There has to be a certain degree of familiarity visible between us or nobody is ever going to believe that we're lovers,' Dante countered with reluctant amusement.

Belle hadn't thought of that aspect of their pretend relationship and she wanted to kick herself for not thinking of it sooner because she had literally walked blind into a brick wall.

'You seem very…nervous,' Dante selected, scrutinising her troubled face with a growing frown. 'I may want you but I promise that I'm not going to try to force you into anything you don't want.'

Belle flushed and straightened her spine, embarrassed that she had made him feel that he had to give her that reassurance. 'I know. But to be honest, er… I'm a bit out of my depth with you.'

'How?' Dante shifted lithely back into his corner, teeth gritting at the biting ache of unfulfillment nagging at him.

'I haven't got a lot of experience,' Belle admitted stiffly. 'I probably should've said no sooner.'

'How much is "not a lot"?' Dante prompted drily.

Belle sucked in a steadying breath. 'I'd rather not go into that.'

'You needn't be shy, nor should you feel that you have to lie for my benefit,' Dante murmured loftily. 'I see women as equals. I *prefer* experienced partners.'

'Well, then, I wouldn't suit you at all!' Belle confided in a tone of stark relief. 'I haven't had a, er, partner yet.'

That statement disconcerted Dante so much that for a split second he simply frowned down at her with astonished dark golden eyes. 'You *can't* be a virgin!'

As he spoke the door beside him was abruptly opened by the driver and both of them were taken by surprise, neither of them having noticed that the car had stopped, and Belle was miraculously rescued from the need to respond to his incredulous statement. In his wake, she slid along the back seat, struggling to keep the skirt of her dress from lifting as she alighted. In what had to be her worst nightmare, just as she was attempting to keep her underwear choices a secret known only to her, the flashbulbs of cameras went off, blinding and disorientating her as she fought to climb out gracefully in her high heels. Mercifully, Dante saved her from a clumsy exit by reaching down to grab her hand with his and he practically pulled her up and out of the limo, giving her the chance to find her feet and discreetly smooth down her rucked frock.

In the crowded entrance foyer, so impervious to the presence of the photographers that he hadn't even spared them a glance, Dante stared broodingly down at her and said again, proving that his mind was still on the conversation she had gratefully abandoned, 'You can't be...'

And Belle's second-worst nightmare came true with those words. She felt the awful burn of that hot familiar tide of colour sweeping up her body in a mortifying tide.

'And a blushing one,' Dante pronounced in even greater disbelief. 'You're supposed to be as much of an urban legend as unicorns.'

CHAPTER THREE

'WE'RE NOT GOING to discuss this any more,' Belle told Dante heatedly as they were ushered through a crowded room of staring diners to a well-lit velvet-lined booth in the corner.

'Don't kid yourself. When you said we had to know stuff about each other, that is definitely something a man would *need* to know,' Dante fielded grimly.

'Not in our situation, it's not,' Belle argued. 'We're only faking it.'

'What would you know about faking it?' Dante enquired witheringly.

'Stop it!' Belle hissed between clenched teeth in a sharp aside before she took a seat. 'If you don't stop embarrassing me, I'll look like a tomato all evening!'

'You could've told me the truth upfront!' Dante replied, still pointed in tone as he spread

open the wine list, signalled the hovering maî-
tre d' and ordered wines in fluent French.

Belle pressed the cool backs of her hands
to her cheeks in an effort to ratchet down her
inner heat source. '*Why* should I have told
you?'

'I feel short-changed and like I'm about to
throw a baby into a snake pit!' Dante groaned
in frustration, wondering if he had chosen the
wrong woman entirely for the role. 'You are
manifestly unsuited to pretending to be my
sexy lover. How on earth are you going to
pull that off?'

'You don't have to have sex to be sexy,' Belle
whispered vehemently across the table. 'Not
five minutes ago you were all over me!'

'If I'd been all over you, we'd still have been
in the limo and I wouldn't be in need of a cold
shower,' Dante parried drily. 'I kissed you.
Let's not get lost in virginal exaggeration.'

'Just *lose* that word from your vocabulary!'
Belle tossed, taking refuge behind her menu
and making hasty selections, desperate to

change the subject. 'It embarrasses me. I wish I'd lied now.'

Dante ordered the food and lounged back in his chair, narrowed sardonic dark eyes welding to her still-flushed face. 'So, tell me why… Religious scruples?'

'My grandparents didn't encourage me to go out and about when I was younger because we lived in a rough area and they were worried about my safety. Then I was restricted by having to stay home as a carer. It wasn't a conscious decision, but lack of opportunity is certainly part of it,' Belle acknowledged, gratefully sipping the water poured for her, soothing her tight vocal cords. 'And that's all I've got to say on the subject.'

'I'm still not satisfied,' Dante admitted, tasting the wine and indicating that it could be poured.

'It's absolutely none of your business,' she told him quietly when they were alone again.

'You made it my business when you made me want you,' Dante contradicted ruefully. 'Now it seems clear that you're one of those women who decides to stay as pure as the driven snow until she marries.'

'I didn't say that I was saving myself for marriage,' Belle pointed out. 'And I'm not. But I only want intimacy if it comes with a serious relationship.'

'I won't offer you a serious relationship.'

'Of course not,' Belle conceded. 'Anyway, I'm working for you, so there won't be anything of that nature to worry about.'

Dante reminded himself that he too had believed at the outset of their agreement that there was no room for sex in it. But from the minute he had touched her, something had indisputably changed for him. He had acknowledged that he wanted her, and all his reservations had vanished at the same moment, which he supposed made him a fairly typical male, driven by his libido. He didn't want her to be out of reach, he didn't want to hear that she would only share a bed with a man if she was in a serious relationship and he was still wondering how she would stand up to Krystal, who oozed sex appeal.

'I'm just waiting to meet the right person,' Belle extended quietly, hoping to defuse the tension with that admission.

'And what is that right person going to be like?' Dante asked with helpless curiosity.

'Someone who matches me. Look, I don't want to talk about this any more. It's too private and personal,' Belle told him abruptly. 'Subject closed.'

Frustration gusted through Dante. 'I suppose you mean someone crazy about dogs.'

'That wouldn't be the most important thing, no,' she countered uncomfortably. 'I accept that I'll have to compromise, and that one person can't possibly meet all my expectations.'

'I suppose you have a list drawn up for that too,' Dante guessed. 'A shopping list of requirements.'

'I'm not shopping.' Belle lifted her chin.

Silence fell. The first course arrived and they ate. By the arrival of the next, Belle had relaxed again, refusing to think about what Dante thought of her because it wasn't important. Like a shooting star, he would only be in her life for a very short space of time and it would be foolish to start worrying about his opinion of her because ultimately it didn't matter, she told herself firmly. No doubt she sounded old-fashioned and naïve to him, but she knew what she wanted and needed and she wasn't about to apologise for it.

'You haven't told me a thing about yourself yet,' she reminded him quietly.

'Background…' Dante shifted a shoulder in a dismissive shrug. 'I'm twenty-eight. My family made their fortune in banking. My father married my mother because she is the daughter of a prince and he was born a prince. They set a very high value on their titles even though the Italian Republic no longer recognises those titles. They had two children because they wanted a son to inherit the title— the heir and the spare. I was the spare,' Dante explained tightly, his sensual mouth twisting at the designation. 'There was a lot of pressure on my brother, Cristiano, to be exactly what my parents wanted him to be. So he went into the bank because they demanded it of him even though it wasn't what he wanted to do with his life.'

'And what about you?' Belle whispered. 'What did they want from you?'

'They barely took notice of my existence. I was simply insurance in case anything ever happened to my older brother,' Dante admitted. 'And tragically, the worst happened. Cristiano messed up an investment fund at the bank. Instead of coming to me for advice and help, and feeling unable to face our parents' criticism, he took an overdose…and then he was gone.'

Belle had paled. His pain at that admission had tightened every muscle in his lean, darkly handsome face and his strain was painfully evident. 'I'm so sorry, Dante.'

'Do you know what my parents said to me at his funeral?' Dante breathed in a raw undertone. 'That he was never meant to *be* the elder son, that he was utterly unsuited to the responsibility and that *I* would be much stronger in the role. They didn't grieve for him because as far as they were concerned he was a social embarrassment and a screw-up.'

'That's awful,' Belle murmured urgently, reaching for his hand, which had clenched into a fist on the tabletop, and smoothing her fingers gently over his. 'They can't possibly have meant it!'

'Oh, they meant it all right,' Dante contradicted with hard conviction as he pushed his plate away with his free hand. 'I wasn't surprised but I'll never get over the guilt because I *could've* saved him.'

'How?' she exclaimed in surprise at the claim.

'*I* could have stepped in and taken over at the bank. I was better qualified. *I* could have made the socially acceptable marriage and provided the next generation. Instead I did what I wanted to do and left him to sink or swim. The best advice I had to offer was for him to walk away but he didn't have the heart to do that because he was desperate, always *desperate*, for our parents' approval,' he completed gruffly.

'That's not your fault. He did what he had to do, and you did what you had to do. Whatever happened, one of you was going to be unhappy, and as your older brother he chose to take the hit,' she reasoned ruefully.

'Let's move on to something less contentious,' Dante murmured, taken aback that he had told her so much and disconcerted by the shimmer of sympathetic tears in her big violet eyes. She was the touchy-feely type just as Cristiano had been and being that way inclined, being vulnerable, was like sticking your head up above the parapet to invite a punch in the face.

'Yes, tell me about where you went to school… and I suppose you went to university,' Belle said, unsurprised by his nod of confirmation. 'We'll just stick to easy facts, the sort of stuff I should know about you.'

The rest of the meal went surprisingly well and by the time they were climbing back into the limo, Belle felt calm enough to ignore the single lingering paparazzo with a camera, who stole another shot of them together.

'Your favourite colour?' she pressed Dante again.

'I don't have one.'

'Everyone has one.'

'Blue… You dressed in blue,' Dante said teasingly, highly amused by her interest in trivia like his birthdate, his favourite foods and sports, none of which he considered remotely important or likely to be of use to her. 'Blue brings out your eyes. I'm going to have to buy you some jewellery. Don't men who live with women buy them jewellery as gifts?'

Belle wrinkled her nose. 'Oh, don't spend any more, for goodness' sake! I'll only be leaving it behind me. I couldn't possibly accept jewellery as part of the deal…unless you could buy fakes,' she suggested, looking at him with sudden hope. 'There are very good fakes around now.'

'I'm not putting you in fakes!' Dante told her, studying her with incredulous dark golden eyes. *Madre di Dio*… You haven't got the sense you were born with, have you?'

Her brow furrowed. 'What do you mean by that?'

'Because a woman wanting to feather her nest would never ever suggest that I buy her fake diamonds. She would want and expect the real thing, even if it was just to sell it at a later date,' he pointed out drily.

'But I'm *not* out to feather my own nest,' Belle argued, her colour heightening. 'I'll be more than content to be paid at the end of this. Anything more than giving me the means to go home and get my life started again would be excessive.'

'Allow me to decide what is excessive.' Dante surveyed her with mounting hunger, his attention lingering on the smooth satiny skin below her throat while he imagined putting his mouth there before toying at his leisure with the sultry curve to her lower lip. He marvelled at how misleading that pouty pink sultriness was.

She was a sensual, sexy woman in denial of her nature and she was saving herself up for some no doubt imaginary and perfect hero, who would disappoint her. The idea of Belle being disappointed galled Dante and he asked himself why when he deemed disappointment to be one of life's certainties. Like his current desire for her, he ruminated sardonically. He imagined that once he had her, he would no longer want her. And wasn't that exactly why he should leave her alone and untouched? He frowned because that little moral question reminded him very much of his brother, who had always been kinder and less ruthless than Dante. When had he ever had *anything* in common with Cristiano apart from the blood in their veins?

CHAPTER FOUR

'I'M PLANNING TO have a drink,' Dante announced when they walked back into the hotel suite. 'Do you want one?'

'No, thanks.' Belle wandered restively round the room. 'I wonder how Charlie's doing.'

'He's doing fine. I got a text and a photo earlier. He's eaten and settled in for the night. I meant to mention it,' Dante asserted, tugging out his phone.

Belle darted over to him and stared down at the photo of Charlie in what looked like a very comfortable dog run. He was snuggled up, nose to tail, in a well-padded dog bed. 'He looks sad,' she sighed. 'Have you any photos of your brother's dogs?'

'I'm afraid not.'

'Why didn't you try to find them a new home?' Belle asked ruefully.

'Cristiano left me a letter. He wanted me to keep them.'

'Yes, but he probably assumed you'd keep them at home with you,' Belle pointed out and then winced. 'Sorry, forget I said that. It was totally tactless.'

'But spot on,' Dante fielded, pouring himself what he imagined would only be his first hard drink of the night. 'Go to bed. I feel like drowning my sorrows.'

'I can't leave you down here alone when you're feeling bad!' Belle protested with a troubled look in her eyes.

'Of course, you can,' Dante asserted. 'I'm not a child you have to worry about.'

She wondered if he had ever got to be a child secure in the love of his parents. They hadn't sounded very loving towards him and his brother. It made her look back on all the years that she had felt sorry for herself because she had neither a father nor a mother who loved her. Yet all along she had had her grandparents loving and supporting her, making up in every way they could for her parents' lack of interest.

'From what you've said about him, I don't think your brother would've wanted you feeling this way,' she murmured uncertainly, fearful of intruding too much.

'And what would you know about it?' Dante derided.

'Nothing,' she agreed apologetically. 'But if he was a kind person, he wouldn't have wanted you beating yourself up about what can't be changed.'

And that was perfectly true, Dante acknowledged grudgingly. Cristiano had always been an optimist who hated dwelling on the darker elements of life. He had made the best of situations, had even tried to make the best he could of the parents he had been born to, tolerating and forgiving their biting scorn and continual demands.

Dante strode forward. 'Stop looking at me with those big sad eyes,' he breathed hoarsely.

'I'm not sad. I just wanted to make you feel better.' Belle sighed.

'Come to bed with me, then. *That* would be guaranteed to make me feel better, *amante*,' Dante growled soft and low, the dark roughened vowel sounds in his voice snaking down her spine like a rough caress.

Belle clashed in consternation with glittering dark golden eyes that made the breath hitch in her tight throat. 'No, that would be a bad idea.'

'Not to my mind,' Dante intoned, catching both her hands in his and tugging her closer. 'You should've got away while you had the chance.'

Her face flamed because she knew that she hadn't wanted to leave him alone. He tempted her as no one ever had and his confession about his brother had made him seem treacherously human and vulnerable, chipping away at her original dislike. It had taught her a lesson too, taught her not to make assumptions about people and assume that wealth cushioned them from the tragedies of life. Going straight to bed, steering clear of spending more time with Dante Lucarelli, would have been the sensible thing to do, but seeing him standing by the windows with a drink in his hand and looking so very alone had bothered her even though there was nothing she could do or say to change anything.

Belle lifted her chin and looked up at him. 'I know you'll let me go if I ask you to.'

'And you won't ask me because you don't *want* me to let you go,' Dante murmured in silken challenge as he trailed a reproving fingertip across a pink cheek, down to the incredibly inviting lush pink of her mouth. 'Well, don't say you weren't warned…'

He leant down and captured her mouth with his, driving her lips apart with the power of his hungry kiss, and she shivered as heat darted through her chilled body, warming every inch of her. She wanted more, she knew she wanted more, knowing that if nothing else when she made no objection to being scooped off her feet and carried over to an armchair where he draped her across his lap without once freeing her mouth again. A quivering intensity of response gripped her as his tongue stroked between her lips to explore.

'The taste of you is sublime,' Dante husked against her throat, his breath see-sawing in and out of his chest. 'But it is also dangerously addictive.'

Belle was amazingly aware of his hand on her thigh, his fingers smoothing below the hem of her dress and moving higher, and she had never wanted anything quite as much as she craved his touch because, even with every muscle in her body taut with denial, a subversive ache between her legs betrayed her with every plundering delve of his tongue. As he skimmed the taut stretch of her panties aside, her fingers speared into his black hair. She didn't know what she was doing, and she didn't care at that moment. Indeed, her only recognisable fear was that he would stop.

And then he touched her, a mere roll of a fingertip against the taut little bud below her mound and her body went haywire, her hips rising in a languorous roll, sweet and frighteningly strong sensation piercing her in a stormy wave. He sat her up and she uttered a little sound of complaint at that moment of disconnection as he unzipped her dress and pulled it down, the unclipped her bra with wicked dexterity so that her unbound breasts tumbled taut and full into his hands.

With a hungry groan, Dante caught a straining pink nipple in his mouth, bending her back over his arm to ravage the bounty he had uncovered. He was fiercely aroused and dimly amused at himself for playing around like a teenager instead of moving single-mindedly from A to Z to extract his own satisfaction as fast as possible. But there was, he was discovering, a shocking satisfaction to be found in her inexperienced responses, in the little gasping sounds she made low in her throat and the increasingly frantic grip of her fingers in his hair. He teased the damp flesh at the heart of her, tracing her body in a caress that almost sent her up in flames in his arms, and then gently exploring to learn that she was even tighter than he had expected.

Belle arched and panted into his mouth,

helpless in his arms, her hips rocking instinctively as the pressure in her pelvis built higher and tightened like a band of steel inside her. She was reaching for that perfect moment, blind, deaf, utterly mindless when with one skilful flick of a finger he sent her flying into the sun. She shuddered and cried out, aftershocks of reaction convulsing her as he curved her up to him to taste her mouth one last time. And for timeless moments she lay there in his arms, ostensibly relaxed by the release of all tension but with her brain already leaping back to life to leave her deeply shaken by what she had allowed to happen.

In an instant she was off his lap, gazing down at him, connecting with brilliant dark, glittering eyes.

'The third time you're in my arms, I *will* be taking you to bed,' Dante murmured slumberously. 'Just putting that warning out there...'

'You know that's not what I want,' Belle began awkwardly, her face burning because she was painfully aware that her behaviour with him was hard to defend.

'You may be a contrary woman, but you want me,' Dante incised with complete assurance.

And he was right, shamelessly, mortifyingly right to the extent that Belle didn't bother staying around to argue with that statement. Her head as high as she could still hold it, she went up to her bedroom and shut the door, a sudden empty hollow feeling assailing her because Dante was still downstairs and every wanton cell in her body wanted him with her. She was learning that nothing was as black and white as she had believed it to be. Desire didn't simply switch off because she didn't want to feel it and desire was a much more significant temptation than she had realised. When Dante kissed her, when Dante held her close, she turned weak and dizzy with longing. Yet longing for and downright *craving* a man who would want nothing more from her than the fleeting pleasure her body could offer him could only lead to *her* unhappiness.

Even so, for the first time she was questioning that she had to love and care for a man before she would have sex with him. Obviously, Dante had no deep feelings for her, and the sense of being close to him that his honesty about his brother's death had awakened in her was dangerously misleading. Was that what had happened to her? Had her sympathy bled over into some strange desire to comfort him that had somehow turned into a sexual invitation? She hadn't meant that to happen and was annoyed that she had failed to call a halt.

Bemusement about her exact motivation and discomfiture over her own conduct kept Belle lying awake for a long time. She accepted that she was discovering stuff about herself with Dante that she would have sooner not known. No matter how hard she tried, she couldn't stamp out her attraction to him, nor could she remain level-headed enough to stay in control in his arms. All she could do now, she reasoned ruefully, was be on her guard and endeavour not to offer Dante any more conflicting signals.

Dante had a cold shower and wondered why he hadn't simply swept Belle straight off to his bed. He was considerably more disturbed by the inexplicable truth that even foreplay with Belle was more exciting than anything he had ever had with another woman. She turned him on, hard and fast, and then she melted with delicious response whenever he touched her. Instead of being furious with her for walking away without giving him the satisfaction he needed, he was already thinking with anticipation about the next time she succumbed to the same hunger that was currently tormenting him. And then maybe *he* would walk away to teach *her* a lesson.

Picturing that scenario, Dante grinned with helpless amusement, knowing that the last thing he would do was walk away. He wouldn't have the self-discipline to walk away because he had let her get under his skin, let her light him up for the first time ever with a fiery need to possess one particular woman. And why was that? Or what was it about her that had penetrated his defences?

What, for instance, had made him talk so very honestly about losing Cristiano? It was true that she would need that background to understand his family set-up and why the land deal was so very important to him. But he had shared details he didn't need to share, drawn out by her warmth and those big compassionate eyes that seemed to offer understanding. In all likelihood it was all an act on her part, he told himself sagely, and she was striving to impress him, possibly hoping to stay in his life for longer than two short weeks.

The following morning, Belle was in a surprisingly good mood. She had behaved foolishly the night before, but she knew that she couldn't turn back time and magically eradicate her mistake. All she could do was avoid getting too close to Dante and start trying to treat him more like her employer. Furthermore, the sun was shining, and she would hopefully be reunited with Charlie soon. More clothing had arrived for her to try and it was a definite treat to skim through the different items and pick a brand-new outfit to wear. She chose a light skirt and top combination, but she frowned at her hair, which was displaying defiant waves again after only one short evening of behaving like her fantasy straight hair. Her true self was fighting to come out again, she thought ruefully, and Dante would just have to accept that she couldn't look perfectly groomed all the time.

'A jeweller is visiting after breakfast,' Dante informed her as she came down the stairs, trying to evade his gaze without being too obvious about it while her colour rose like a banner to advertise her self-consciousness. 'And then we're heading out to shop for furniture and some other items. Tomorrow, we'll fly home to Italy.'

'Why would we need to shop for furniture?' Belle asked as she settled down at the breakfast table with him.

'You're moving in with me. Presumably a woman moving in with a man would have items she wanted to bring with her. You have nothing, so we will have to buy some stuff. I want us to look like an authentic couple, to my staff and everyone else in my life,' Dante admitted calmly. 'That we are only pretending has to remain *our* secret.'

'Charlie's authentic,' Belle pointed out helplessly. 'I am moving in my dog.'

Dante lounged back in his chair to study her. In silk that accentuated the swell of her breasts and somehow enhanced the satiny softness of her pale skin, she looked incredibly sensual and very touchable. He watched as she tucked a stray strand of bright hair behind one small ear and nibbled at her lower lip and reminded himself that seducing her would be cruel, because he was never going to offer her the serious relationship she wanted. He breathed in deep, recognising the erotic pulse gaining strength at his groin, and he shifted position in outright denial of her libidinous effect on him. 'Charlie's not enough on his own. We need to buy you some artworks and some presentable pieces of furniture.'

Her smooth brow furrowed. *'Art?* Why would I need artworks?'

'Part of your new image. You're an art lover like me,' Dante told her.

'Yes, I do like some art,' Belle conceded thoughtfully. 'But not on the sort of level you would admire. I agreed to do this, Dante, but I didn't agree to pretend to be someone I'm not.'

An ebony brow lifted enquiringly. 'Meaning?'

'The relationship may be fake but, while I'm in it, I'm going to be *me*,' Belle informed him stiffly. 'I'm not going to fake being something I'm not, so I don't want fancy artworks or furniture. I'm an ordinary working woman and I wouldn't know where to begin acting as if I was someone much fancier and richer.'

'That's quite a speech and I appreciate the sentiments you express but I don't see what difference it makes in our circumstances.'

'Well, then, you're not listening,' Belle interrupted more sharply. 'I'm me and I'm *staying* me because that way I'm less likely to make mistakes. I've been a housekeeper, a carer and a waitress, and I won't pretend otherwise.'

'And if you're not part of my world, how am I supposed to have met the *real* you?' Dante asked very drily.

'Make it a funny story. I served you in a bar one night? You met me when you visited someone I was looking after or working for... You picked me up when I was hitchhiking? Use your imagination. Maybe you're moving in with me because I'm *different* from the other women you've had in your life. Don't try to make me hide the real me, as if that is something to be ashamed of,' Belle urged ruefully.

'You're very stubborn.'

'And so are you.'

'Consequently, no artworks?' Dante checked with a censorious shake of his arrogant dark head. 'But there has to be some furniture, so that you can turn some room in my house into *your* room... Isn't that what women do when they move in with a man?'

Belle shrugged. 'How would I know? And it's an awful lot of fuss and expense to go to simply to put on an act for one weekend,' she reasoned, searching his lean bronzed features with curiosity sparkling in her dark blue eyes.

'Presumably you think getting this business deal is worth any amount of trouble.'

'Pretty much,' Dante agreed.

'Well, then, if it's just one room I could choose a comfortable chair, a small table, bookshelves…oh, and books,' she added reflectively, her eyes warming at the prospect. 'But brand-new furniture won't look very convincing—'

'We'll buy antiques,' Dante incised in a tone of finality.

'But you're not going to expect me to pretend to be something I'm not?' Belle pressed, seeking reassurance.

'No,' Dante conceded, marvelling that he was giving way on that point for in truth he had planned to set her up with an entire false identity, which would have protected his privacy and her anonymity. 'You appreciate that the media will take a much stronger interest in me hooking up with a waitress?'

'I'll be out of your life again before anyone has even identified me,' Belle parried confidently, lifting her head, vibrant waves of copper-red hair shifting across her shoulders and glinting fierily in the light.

'It goes against the grain to admit it, but I liked your hair better before the beauty consultants in the spa got their hands on you. Curly hair suits you,' Dante framed, already questioning what he was saying and frowning at that unplanned dive into personal comment as he sprang lithely upright to greet the older man with a large leather case and his accompanying security guard being shown into the room. 'Monsieur Duchamp, you are very welcome.'

Belle tugged her fingers down from the hair she had involuntarily been touching. He liked her hair better when it was *au naturel*. Well, what did you know? She was astonished but decidedly flattered.

An hour later, she was sporting a designer watch and bracelet, sapphire-and-diamond earrings and a sapphire-and-diamond pendant, the absolute basics without which Dante had insisted she could not perform her role.

The limousine dropped them on the Carré

Rive Gauche, which was full of antiques dealers and the kind of esoteric shops haunted by interior designers. Belle found herself much more interested in what was on offer there than she had expected to be because the sheer quirkiness of some of the items intrigued her.

'You're seeing stuff that interests you,' Dante noted.

'I like finding out the history behind them… I like that seat,' she said, pointing at an elaborately upholstered and very comfortable-looking low-slung armchair.

The proprietor, quick to recognise Dante for the rich buyer that he was, hastened over to talk about the chair and demonstrated the weird way part of the arms swivelled back at a touch. Their exchange of French was too fast for her to follow and Belle stared up at Dante in surprise as he began to laugh. Poised there with his dark eyes gleaming with intense amusement, his lean, darkly handsome features relaxed, he was so breathtakingly beautiful and male that she couldn't take her eyes off him.

'What's so funny?' Belle whispered.

'I'll tell you later. We're taking the chair... Come on, keep looking,' Dante urged, one long-fingered hand pressing against her taut spine as he walked her along with him. 'You have a whole room to fill and none of the rooms in my home are small.'

A fat sofa, an Indian carved bookcase, a small inlaid table, a beautiful mirror and an eccentric art deco drinks cabinet followed in quick succession.

'And as an ordinary girl, how am I supposed to have acquired all these valuable items?' Belle enquired with reluctant amusement.

'They are all gifts from me,' Dante teased with a smile. 'I've also ordered a selection of English classics and contemporary novels for you from a bookseller.'

In the limo on the way back to the hotel, he told her that he was taking her out for dinner again and then on to a club. Belle was lazily contemplating the options in her new wardrobe when Dante appeared in the doorway.

'Rain check, I'm afraid,' he murmured quietly. 'There's been a fatal accident on one of my wind farms in Brittany and I have to visit the site. I don't know when I'll get back but it could be the early hours. We'll still be flying to Italy in the morning.'

'Fatal?' she queried in dismay.

Dante nodded. 'A construction engineer fell in one of the turbine towers,' he told her grimly.

'That's dreadful. Will you be seeing his family?'

'Yes,' Dante replied gravely. 'And checking out whether or not safety procedures were correctly followed. There'll have to be an enquiry.'

Belle dined in solitary state at the grand dining table, went for a shower and changed into her pyjamas. Before she returned downstairs, she succumbed to curiosity and entered Dante's bedroom. It was scrupulously tidy with no sign of his hasty departure, but she wasn't there to snoop, she was there to check out whether her suspicions were correct. And they were. There *was* a bath in the palatial suite but it was in the bathroom off the master bedroom. It was the bath of her dreams as well, a huge oval tub with a fantastic view of Paris.

Belle had always loved baths, but she hadn't lived anywhere with a bath for several years. Everyone was putting in showers now. Mrs Devenish's family had had her original bath taken out and replaced with a shower in which she could safely sit. Belle had missed treating herself to the luxury of a bath and she wondered if she dared make use of Dante's while he was out but that idea, tempting as it was, struck her as too cheeky and she went back downstairs and watched television instead.

Around ten, the image of that bath overcame her reluctance and, with a sigh of acceptance, she scrambled up, switched off the television and went to take advantage of it. The bathroom was packed with bath preparations in designer pots and she made liberal use of one of them before pinning her hair up in a clasp and climbing in to lower herself slowly into the deliciously scented warm water. Resting her head back on the padded pillow, she sighed, deciding that she was in heaven as she relaxed, truly relaxed for the first time in months.

She realised that she had dozed off only after a noise startled her into wakefulness again. Water sloshing noisily around her, she jerked up into sitting position, needing a moment even to appreciate where she was. Registering that she was *still* in Dante's bathroom, she froze for a split second until she heard quick steps on the wooden stairs and then, swiftly depressing the plug to empty out the water, she launched herself upright in sheer panic. She almost fell as she raced across the slippery tiles to snatch up a big grey towel, winding it round her as fast as she could. She was cursing herself for invading his bathroom, which she had planned to leave immaculate so that no one would even know that she had used it. All hope of that remaining a secret was now gone with water very noisily draining out of the bath and an array of wet footprints and splashes marking the high-shine floor tiles.

Dante was not in a good mood on his return.

Dealing with the man's broken-hearted family had been distressing, and learning that the guy had suffered from vertigo but had concealed it because he had been desperate for a good job had been even less pleasant. And then he saw his bedroom door was lying open and emerging from the en-suite bathroom was a very red-faced Belle, wrapped in a towel and clutching a bundle of clothing to her breasts. She looked so guilty and so embarrassed, it was comical.

'What on earth are you doing in here?' Dante intoned in wonderment, trying very hard not to laugh.

Belle hopped off one bare foot onto the other. 'Your room has a bath… Mine doesn't. I didn't think you'd mind if you weren't here… but I didn't get around to cleaning up, I'm afraid, because I wanted to be out of here before you caught me.'

'And look how well that turned out,' Dante commented.

'I'll come straight back and clean up once I've got dressed,' she told him apologetically, her face on fire. 'I swear I wasn't snooping or anything. That's probably what you think but I didn't touch or look at anything in here. I just missed having baths and I was tempted.'

As Dante was tempted, appraising her curvy little body in the towel, noting how the tight hold she had on the clothing merely accentuated the magnificent swell of her breasts over the towel. Pale, lightly speckled flesh that he had already touched and tasted, and which had only ignited his hunger for more of the experience. Her hair was piled up in a glorious curly mass, innumerable little tendrils escaping to accentuate the flushed oval of her face, dominated by huge violet eyes and that glorious mouth. It was every fantasy Dante had ever had of her rolled into one and he went instantly hard. She was also the distraction he badly needed after the evening he had endured.

'You look amazing,' he told her gruffly because she did, all bright and flushed and embarrassed in her bare feet but somehow, for all her diminutive size, extraordinarily vibrant, full of life and sass.

'I hardly think so... You're a guy, it's probably just the bath towel,' she deflected tautly, because she was painfully aware that she wanted him to mean what he had said.

'No, it's you...all you,' Dante husked, logic kicking in to demolish his reservations and neatly shift him to where he wanted to be. As they had both acknowledged, it wasn't a normal job that he had given her, and it would also be an extremely temporary one. 'Forget the rules about what you should and shouldn't do, ditch the lists and the expectations. Just *be* with me because you *want* to be.'

Belle was rigid with tension and then a little quiver ran through her, her breathing quickening. She hadn't expected him to be that bold, hadn't been prepared for him to strip everything back to the basics.

'Live a little.' Dante leant back against the door to close it before crossing the room to gently pull the bundle of clothing out of her too-tight hold and drop it to the floor.

'But I'm *working* for you,' she began urgently as she clutched at the precarious towel to ensure that it didn't fall.

'Any court in Europe would deny that our private arrangement has anything in common with a normal job, which is why we shouldn't feel bound by stupid rules,' he argued impatiently. 'Those rules don't apply to our situation and we don't need to consider them.'

Live a little, he had said, and he could not know how deeply those words affected her because Belle was unhappily conscious that she had barely lived at all during her twenty-two years on earth. She had missed out on the supposedly fun-filled years of teenaged experimentation and had felt old before her time dealing with major responsibilities like terminal illness, household bills on a small budget and bereavement. With elderly grandparents, she had always had to be sensible and there had been an awful lot of rules to follow. Rules she was *still* faithfully following, she acknowledged ruefully.

'I know I'm not that guy on your shopping

list whom you would choose,' Dante murmured. 'But right now, I'm the one that you *want…*'

And the mad cacophony of warning voices in her head telling her to back away, go to her own bed and sensibly turn her back on the risk he presented, suddenly went silent. Yes, he was the one she wanted, the only one she had ever wanted, and all of a sudden holding out for that one perfect match of a guy who might never come along seemed spineless and sad. Dante had smashed through her defences because the bottom line was undisputable… *I'm the one that you want.*

'That's true,' she framed shakily.

'And it is equally true that I want you,' Dante breathed, bending down to lift her up and settle her down on the bed. 'Let's not make it more complicated than that.'

CHAPTER FIVE

BUT IT *WAS* much more complicated than that, Belle thought helplessly as she watched Dante tugging loose his tie, shrugging free of his jacket. Where did they go from here? Was this a one-night stand, as it was called? Would they move on and act as if it had never happened for the duration of their time together? Would one act of sex kill the attraction between them? How was she supposed to know?

She was lying in a damp towel on a bed and common sense was telling her to throw it off, but she didn't feel brave enough for that. Although she had been half-naked in his arms the night before, that had been different, and her lack of self-consciousness had been entirely due to the heat of the moment when no thought had been required from her and no single sensible thought had occurred to her.

No, Belle was very much aware that such thoughts came afterwards, and nervous tension held her fast with Dante providing a very welcome distraction as he stripped.

He was very fit, she conceded numbly, sentenced to silence by awe and shyness as rippling bands of muscle sheathed in bronzed skin began to appear. He shed his shirt, toed off his shoes, peeled off socks, his sleek muscular development on continual display as he flexed and turned and straightened, his trousers hanging low on his lean hips, an intriguing ribbon of dark hair snaking down his flat stomach and disappearing beneath the waistband. He was beautiful, like some flawless fantasy brought to life in the flesh, she reflected, shutting her eyes circumspectly as the trousers slid down. She had felt his arousal, noticed, but she wasn't going to stare while he was watching her like a hawk. Those clever dark golden eyes didn't miss a trick and she didn't want to embarrass herself and be guilty of doing that blushing-virgin thing that he had already mocked.

* * *

'You're as quiet as a mouse,' Dante whispered, tugging gently at the edge of the towel as she held on to it. He was as aroused as hell and fighting to stay in control.

'There's too many lights on in here,' she told him, violet eyes flying wide.

Without a word, Dante reached up and dimmed the lights to a more acceptable level. 'Better?'

Belle nodded jerkily. Now that he was actually on the bed, naked and ready to proceed, nerves were swallowing her alive.

'I want you to be sure about this,' Dante breathed abruptly. 'I don't want you sharing this bed with me if you're going to regret it. I don't want to take advantage of you.'

'I know you don't...' Involuntarily, Belle lifted her hand to his lean, darkly handsome face and ran soothing fingers across his brow, where he was frowning, her fingertips skating up into his silky black hair, smoothing down the tousled strands.

It was the warmth she emanated, Dante recognised in consternation. That was what had made him spill his guts the night before, that seemingly natural warmth and affection that had broken through his habitual reserve. That discovery about her and about himself, that he could actually be *that* impressionable, *that* easily influenced by a woman, unnerved him. Yet, in defiance of all the defensive instincts that urged him to back off and steer clear of such manipulation until he could get a better handle on it, he still leant down and kissed her as though his life depended on it.

From zero to ninety in seconds, she thrummed into life like a well-primed engine, Belle thought dizzily as he ravaged her parted lips with the kind of hunger that set her on fire. A jolt of high-voltage electricity shot through her, ensuring she was aware of every inch of her pulsing body and every point of contact where his hot, muscular body connected with hers.

'This is the very best moment of my day, *cara mia*,' Dante confided, undoing the clasp in her hair and tossing it aside before fanning out the tangle of her curls round her face.

The towel was gone and she hadn't noticed it going, Belle registered in dismay as a lean hand travelled up over her ribcage to mould a pale, pouting breast, catching a straining pink nipple between thumb and finger to massage it in a way that sent little tremors down to her pelvis, ensuring that she became insanely conscious of the damp heat blooming there.

He used his tongue to tease her sensitive nipples and the little tremors picked up pace as he sucked on the swollen buds. Her hips shifted upward of their own volition and he flattened her to the mattress with the force of a sudden demanding kiss. Her hands went into his hair and locked there as he ground his hips into her, sending need rocketing up through her in a heady surge. Her body strained up to his and, by then, all her anxiety had fled because nothing had ever felt so necessary, so right or so good. Even the scent of him, dark and masculine laced with a spicy cologne that had already become familiar to her, was compelling.

He shimmied down the length of her, lean

and lithe, parting her thighs, burying his mouth there with a fervour for that intimacy that shocked her. 'You taste so good,' he husked while she trembled all over with reaction, torn between wanting him to stop and wanting him to continue.

As exquisite sensation seduced her, she fought to stay in control, to stop panting for breath, to stop making little noises she couldn't restrain and to still the urge to simply writhe. The pleasure was all-consuming, like a slow burn rising from the heart of her with his every spellbinding caress. Pulsating bands of tension tightened round the dull ache of need at the very heart of her, driving it higher until it peaked and set fireworks rocketing inside her, her whole body convulsing in physical delight.

'If this hurts too much, I'll stop,' Dante swore, sliding over her, tipping her legs back. 'Just tell me.'

'OK,' Belle mumbled, still semi-lost in the waves of bliss that had engulfed her as she felt his surge against her, hard and determined where she was soft and tender and yet, oh, so ready for him. There wasn't a doubt in her head about what she was doing at that moment, not with everything feeling so new and fresh and Dante's experience soothing her insecurities. His dark eyes were pure golden enticement as they held hers.

She skated her hands up and down over his smooth brown shoulders, enjoying the satiny strength of him while irresistible sensation snaked through her as he slowly entered her, stretching her sensitive body. She quivered as the heat of excitement clenched her again and then a stabbing pain hit, and she gasped and he stopped dead.

'I'm hurting you.'

'No, don't stop!' she exclaimed.

'Then try to relax. The more you tense, the tougher the challenge is,' he rasped.

Every nerve in her body still stirred to an edge of breathless excitement, she struggled to relax, and he moved again and it still hurt but this time she buried her face in his shoulder and bore the discomfort in silence. Mercifully, it was fleeting, and she heard his groan of satisfaction as he plunged deeper into her and somehow that lit her up as if she had a thousand-watt bulb burning somewhere inside her.

Her heart rate accelerated as the excitement conquered her again and shot higher with every plunge of his lean hips. A kind of wildness claimed her, and she wrapped her legs round him, urging him on as he pounded into her to finally assuage that insane ache of hungry need at the heart of her. She cried out as the ripples of another climax coursed through her and the wild, sizzling pleasure sent her spinning into release. Dante shuddered over her with a harsh groan of masculine satisfaction and the world went still for her then.

'Unbelievable,' Dante growled, rolling over and carrying her with him, golden eyes as bright as if flames burned there as he stared down at her. 'That was unbelievable. Are you OK?'

Not feeling up to the challenge of speech or voicing an opinion, Belle nodded.

Dante gazed down at her and smoothed her hair with an unholy grin. 'Your hair looks like I electrified it, *amante mia.*'

He had electrified *her.* Belle gave him a drowsy smile. 'It's called bed hair and it's like that every morning when I wake up.'

'I love your hair,' Dante told her carelessly as he rolled off the bed and headed for the bathroom.

'Where do we go from here?' Belle asked abruptly before she could think better of it.

Dante froze and suppressed a groan, knowing that he should have foreseen that question and should not have overlooked her inexperience. She wanted to know what came next when nobody got to know what came next, he reasoned in frustration. Even so, with him what came next after bedding a woman was usually predictable. He would get bored and move on and she would go home.

'We go on as we have begun,' Dante responded gruffly. 'I'll run you another bath.'

Belle was bewildered. *We go on as we have begun.* What was that supposed to mean?

After all, they had *begun* as strangers agreeing to a platonic arrangement. Was he suggesting that they now return to that? And how was she supposed to ask him for further clarification? *That* would make her look a little desperate for reassurance and probably potentially clingy to a man already wary of clingy women. Furthermore, what was the protocol after such an encounter? Should she get up and return to her own room? If he expected that, he wouldn't be running a bath for her, she told herself irritably and smothered a yawn, too sleepy and comfortable to want to move.

'We have a problem,' Dante informed her from the bathroom doorway, something in his voice, something spooked, cutting through her relaxation to make her take notice and push herself up on one elbow.

'The condom tore,' Dante completed grimly.

Belle pushed an uncertain hand through the tousled strands of red and copper spilling across her white brow, her violet eyes stricken, her freckles standing out in contrast to her pallor. *'Tore?'* she repeated shakily.

'It can happen,' Dante breathed tautly, his strong bone structure taut below his bronzed skin. 'But it's never happened to me before. Possibly I was a little too passionate. Are you on any form of contraception?'

Belle went pink. 'Why would I have been?'

Dante shrugged. 'I had to ask. Sometimes women use birth control for other reasons,' he pointed out without any expression at all, and then he turned on his heel and vanished back into the bathroom.

Belle was frozen where she sat and then, in an abrupt movement, she slid out of the bed, wincing at the ache between her thighs, her newly extreme awareness that she had had sex for the first time… And what a disastrous mistake that impulsive and seemingly daring decision was now starting to seem, she reflected wretchedly. It had not even occurred to her that she could use birth control simply to be prepared for such an event. But naturally she had never dreamt that she would end up just falling into bed with someone like Dante. She had assumed that she would be in a serious relationship before she had sex and that there would be time and space to consider such precautions. And why was that?

Because nobody knew *better* than Belle, who was illegitimate and the supposed result of a contraceptive accident, that chance pregnancies should be carefully guarded against and that even the possibility of a child should always be planned to the nth degree.

Belle's father, Alastair Stevenson, hadn't wanted her... For goodness' sake, *neither* of her parents had wanted her! Alastair had had a brief affair with her mother and they had broken up by the time Tracy approached her former lover to tell him that she had conceived. Tracy had sworn that she was pregnant due to a contraceptive failure, but Belle's father had made it painfully obvious to Belle, aged a mere thirteen at their only meeting, that he suspected her mother's pregnancy had been no accident. And in all fairness to Alastair, Belle, knowing Tracy as she did, would have been suspicious too, because it was perfectly possible that, having set her sights on him, her scheming mother had deliberately conceived in an attempt to entrap a well-heeled husband.

Pale as milk, Belle wrapped her clammy body in the discarded towel and dropped down on the foot of the disordered bed, deeply shaken at the mere idea that she had run the risk of falling pregnant. And the last thing she wanted to do was raise a child alone with the father having absolutely no interest in his child. It had done nothing for her self-respect to be confronted by a father who couldn't care less about her, and who indeed seemed to resent her for the simple fact that she had even been born, costing him a small fortune in child-support payments…not that her rich father, a highly successful banker by all accounts, could have found it that much of a challenge to make those payments.

Dante was grateful for the distraction of running the bath. He had never done such a thing for a woman before but felt the effort was required after his less-than-stellar taking of her virginity, which he had hoped to accomplish without hurting her. He was tense and distracted though, already asking himself why he hadn't gone ahead and had a vasectomy when the idea had first occurred to him some years earlier. Cristiano had talked him out of that idea. But Dante absolutely refused to give his parents the heir they craved to ensure the next generation of their precious dynasty. And they had been such dreadful parents that he was convinced he would be equally hopeless in the same role. That was why he had never wanted a child. He lacked heart and affection.

But what if he *had* got Belle pregnant? What would she want to do in such circumstances? If she was even half as fond of children as she was of that scruffy little dog she would want to go ahead and have the child. And then, whether he liked it or not, he would be a father with all a father's responsibilities.

'Your bath's ready,' Dante murmured from the doorway. 'I'm going for a shower.'

Belle stood up. 'What will we do if—'

'We'll deal with it…*if* it happens,' Dante countered levelly, his dark golden eyes veiled. 'There's no point fretting about it right now.'

* * *

There was a lot of sense in that wait-and-see attitude, Belle told herself as she settled down into the bath, unable to relax into its warmth because she was too tense and far too busy watching Dante's arrogant dark head shift behind the marble wall that closed off the shower. She supposed she might have considered the morning-after pill had she not been so aware that, had such an option been available to her mother, Tracy, she herself would never have been born at all. And that was a very sobering thought. When Alastair Stevenson had refused to marry Tracy as she had hoped, any interest her mother had had in her unborn child had vanished. Indeed, Tracy had resented being left as an unwed mother and had resented even more the damage pregnancy had done to her previously perfect figure, and she had taken that bitterness out on her daughter.

Belle didn't stay long in the bath. In fact, she crept out of the bathroom like a cat burglar, dropped her towel and donned her pyjamas in frantic haste to get back to her own bedroom as quickly as she possibly could. After all, if there had been an ambience between them, it had died after the mishap. His shuttered face had told her all she would ever need to know about Dante's opinion of her having his child. He didn't want it to happen. He didn't even want to think about such a possibility. And in that, she supposed, he wasn't much different from any other young single guy put in the same position. How else could she expect him to feel? It wasn't as if he were in love with her. It wasn't as if he even knew her that well.

Her dispirited eyes took in the opulence of her bedroom and she sighed. It wasn't even as if she and Dante came from the same world. She was a girl with a mother and a father who ignored her, only casual friends, and she had been sleeping in a rusty campervan and working as a waitress when Dante had met her. Dante was a guy who travelled in limos, wore incredibly elegant designer suits and he had spent more than half his life being educated. She was a nobody, a nothing in comparison, she decided wretchedly.

Why, oh, why had she slept with him? Why had she let herself be tempted like that? *Live a little? Live a little and live to regret it*, she concluded unhappily...

CHAPTER SIX

DANTE HAD BEEN up working since the crack of dawn when Belle finally showed.

She gave him a huge smile from the top of the stairs when their eyes met. It was fake as hell and he liked that he could tell that it was fake because she had a highly expressive face. Faint shadows highlighted her violet eyes and proved that she had not slept much better than he had. Served her right for leaving his bed the way she had, he reflected, dark golden eyes simmering. Dante wasn't used to women taking him by surprise or making moves on their own, and Belle had done both when he had found her gone when he'd got out of the shower the night before. Well, she wouldn't be doing that tonight, he thought with innate satisfaction, because she would only be sleeping in *his* bed while she was in Italy.

'You have about thirty minutes to get breakfast,' Dante murmured softly, watching the sunlight make a fiery halo of her hair and add sparkle to her eyes. Her outfit—striped cropped trousers and a white top, teamed with canvas sneakers—had a nautical air that gave her the look of a sexy sailor. His keen gaze roamed over her shapely figure and he remembered that she had felt like liquid silk and he hardened instantly.

'I'm starving,' Belle admitted unselfconsciously as she dropped down into a seat and the butler appeared to take her order. 'I can hardly wait to be reunited with Charlie.'

'We'll pick him up on the way home. By the way, I've arranged for your packing to be done.'

Belle nodded and smiled as a pot of tea arrived. She was disturbingly aware of the lingering scrutiny of Dante's stunning dark golden eyes. What was he watching and waiting for? She had agreed with his wait-and-see outlook and she wasn't about to freak out over something that might never happen. At the same time, she had had thoughts during the night that would probably horrify Dante because she had tried to imagine herself becoming a mother. For someone who had never had a mother as such that had been a scary prospect, but she had decided that she would cope, somehow, she would cope the way she always had when life threw up unexpected developments.

And the more she had thought about how different a parent she would be in comparison to her own parents, the more she had warmed to the vague image of a baby she could love. A little boy, a little girl, she didn't care, but she *did* like children and the idea of finally having her own family could only warm her heart. That was the right attitude to have, she told herself firmly: turn any negative aspect into a positive so that she was prepared for whatever happened.

'When will we know?' Dante asked levelly.

Belle registered that his mind was in exactly the same place as her own and she coloured. 'In about ten days—'

'We'll have a test done as soon as possible,' Dante told her in the same measured tone.

Belle demolished a croissant in record time, unnerved by Dante's calm and slightly irritated that he was hiding how he really felt from her, acting all distant and businesslike in the aftermath of the passionate encounter they had shared the night before. Of course, it would be neither civil nor kind of him to admit that he was horrified by their situation, she allowed grudgingly. Really, *she* was being unreasonable in expecting any more from him than a polite pretence.

Dante watched Belle's lips curl round a shred of croissant, the tip of her tongue peeking out as she savoured the pastry with unconcealed pleasure, her head tipping back slightly, lashes lowering, her white throat exposed, her slim body momentarily stretching, the fabric pulling tight across the full firm swell of her breasts. He was fiercely aroused by her sensual enjoyment of her food and he marvelled at the way she could make the simplest things seem impossibly sexy. Thoroughly disconcerted by his reaction, Dante attempted to work out why having Belle once had only whetted his appetite for her and stoked it higher, instead of at least partially cooling his immediate interest.

Glancing curiously across the table at Dante, who had gone very still, his attention locked to her, his lean, strong jawline clenching hard, Belle muttered, 'What's up?'

'I still want you,' Dante breathed in a driven undertone. 'In fact, if we had the time I'd be hauling you back upstairs right now!'

Eyes widening in astonishment at that bold admission, Belle stared at him and a piece of croissant went down the wrong way. Choking, she gasped and coughed, eyes streaming as she took a drink to clear her tight throat. Well, she guessed she had just got her answer about what happened next, but she hadn't expected to receive it quite so directly.

'I'm a passionate guy. I can't change what I am,' Dante murmured huskily. 'But I'm hoping you feel the same way.'

Belle chewed tautly at the soft fullness of her lower lip and could feel the flames breaking out below her skin, an anticipatory warm dampness flowering between her thighs while her nipples tightened in response. 'Er...yes.'

'You see,' Dante pronounced with satisfaction. 'Nothing between us has to be complicated.'

And she thought, *He can't possibly be so clever and yet so stupid at the same time, can he?* Because their relationship had become extremely complicated, not least because of the contraceptive mishap the day before and his desire to continue their intimacy undeterred by that development.

'You think I'll be more convincing playing your lover if I actually am?' Belle queried.

'If I didn't want you I wouldn't be with you,' Dante said drily. 'And I wanted you the instant I saw you.'

Belle shifted in her seat, helplessly gratified by that admission.

'There had to be chemistry for us to do this,' Dante pointed out. 'I could hardly pretend to be living with a woman who didn't attract me.'

'Obviously not.' Belle squashed down the

urge to ask him how often he saw a woman he immediately wanted in the way he had evidently wanted her. Probably ten or more times a day, she scolded herself ruefully. It bothered her that in his radius she jumped like a fish at a hook, overanalysing his every word, quite unable to re-establish the cool, calm outlook that usually guided her around men.

It was different with Dante; *she* was different with Dante. He was *more* in every way than every other man she had ever met, better looking, smarter, more sophisticated and unarguably richer. She recognised her subconscious wish that she was something more special to him than a passing fancy and she almost grimaced with self-loathing. There was no future in their arrangement and the last thing she needed to do was start getting attached to him or developing unrealistic expectations. Cinderella rarely got her prince in the real world.

'Those who know me will be surprised enough that I have moved a woman into my home with me,' Dante admitted, raking impatient fingers through his unruly black hair. 'I have always been very forthright about my lack of interest in marriage and my desire to retain my freedom. So, as a couple, we do *have* to put on a convincing show.'

'You're making me more and more curious about this business deal that is so important to you,' Belle confided. 'It must be something pretty special to make you go to these lengths to attain it.'

'Krystal's husband, Eddie, owns a piece of land that I hope to reclaim.'

Belle frowned. 'Reclaim?' She questioned his choice of that word.

'The land used to belong to my brother and he was very attached to it. My parents sold it off when I was abroad on business because they're not sentimental people.'

'Couldn't you have bought the land direct from them?' she asked.

'No, they would have made other demands of me. I don't put myself in a vulnerable position with them,' he replied in a guarded tone, glancing across the room in relief as a collection of suitcases on a trolley were wheeled towards the lift. 'I believe it's time for us to leave.'

Dante worked during the flight, barely lifting his head from his laptop. Belle pondered the situation she was about to enter, the 'snake pit' as Dante had referred to it as. An array of un-appealing characters awaited her, it seemed, the nasty parents, the clingy troublemaking ex from hell. But no, when he didn't get on well with his parents, she would hardly be dragged out to meet them, she reasoned, striking his titled parents from the list of challenges ahead. Instead she concentrated on her reunion with Charlie.

The cluster of shouting and gesticulating press-waving cameras as they emerged from the VIP channel at the airport came as a rude wake-up call. 'Look happy,' Dante urged in her ear as he locked a supportive hand to her stiff spine. Belle smiled and all the cameras obediently flashed. He didn't pause to respond to the questions being hurled at him. Security guards escorted them out to the waiting limousine.

'You're clearly quite a celebrity in Italy. You should've mentioned that,' Belle told him.

'Gossip columnists take a ridiculous interest in my private life and for once I've given them something to report…thanks to you.'

'What have *I* got to do with it?' Belle demanded.

'You insisted that you be allowed to be yourself and I have given you your wish. When my staff were asked to identify you, they admitted that you were a waitress I met in France and the press do love to wallow in a whirlwind romance,' Dante declared with cynical amusement.

'I just wasn't expecting *that* level of public interest in your life,' Belle told him, already beginning to regret her insistence that she go under her own name with Dante as she wondered if her father would read about her in some newspaper.

On the other hand, she couldn't imagine her father reading a gossip column, but what did

she know about the man? Very little and hopefully any publicity would be confined to the
Italian press. Yet her self-respect cringed at the
possibility of her father learning that she had
moved in with a very rich Italian because he
would no doubt assume that she was faithfully
following in her gold-digging mother's footsteps. And she didn't want to give her long-
absent father the excuse to believe that he had
been *right* not to pursue a more normal relationship with her. His rejection and the injus-
tice of being held accountable for her mother's
sins still stung.

Charlie greeted her with rapture at the smart
boarding kennels, bounding into her arms as
if they had been parted for months. She petted
him and calmed him down before turning to
Dante to say, 'Let's go and say hello to your
brother's dogs while we're here.'

Dante frowned. 'I don't think…'

'Don't be mean, Dante,' Belle argued fierily. 'Imagine how boring it must be in here for
them every day and how much it will mean to
them to get a visit.'

Incredulous at being called mean for the first time in his life, Dante spread lean brown hands in frustration and annoyance. 'Five minutes… that's all,' he specified. 'And that's all you'll want because they're frantic little beasts with no manners at all.'

'We'll put Charlie into his travelling box and leave him out here while we visit them. It wouldn't be fair to unsettle them with a strange dog,' Belle remarked as she persuaded Charlie into the box. 'You know, Dante…dogs can learn manners. With a little training, you might find them perfectly acceptable. I'm willing to help if I can.'

'They're *not* coming home with us,' Dante swore vehemently, registering that when he gave an inch with Belle she tried to take a mile.

'OK,' Belle conceded, wondering how long it would take to change his mind as he addressed the proprietor and they were led down a corridor giving access to a line of kennels.

'They jump up at you and drop hair everywhere,' Dante complained, angry that he had allowed himself to be shamed into doing something he didn't want to do.

Belle didn't know what breed of dog she had expected Dante's late brother to have owned but she was surprised to see two tiny short-haired chihuahuas, one brown, one black and white, nestled cosily in an extravagant pink basket. As they leapt out of the basket to greet Dante with an enthusiasm he didn't deserve, Belle crouched down and quite deliberately got in their way. In seconds she had an armful of squirming, overexcited chihuahuas in her lap and she sat down on the floor of the corridor below Dante's disbelieving gaze and slowly calmed them down with a quiet voice and an occasional sharp no.

'Do you want to hold them now they've settled?' she asked Dante over her shoulder.

'No,' Dante said flatly.

Belle suppressed a sigh and resisted the temptation to ask him to make an effort. She petted the little animals, wondering how Dante could withstand those little pleading dark eyes. He had been doing it for a year, she reminded herself wryly.

'They've never behaved that well for me,' he confided. 'Clearly, you're the beast whisperer.'

Belle sighed as she returned the dogs to their kennels and they whined and clawed at the mesh in disappointment. 'I suppose I was expecting your brother to have hunting dogs… well, something large and macho.'

'Cristiano was liked cute dogs,' Dante admitted quietly. 'He was gay, and the more our parents criticised him, the more flamboyant he became.'

'They couldn't accept him as he was?'

'Oh, they're very liberal and accepting in public, and they have gay friends, but they still didn't want a gay eldest son and heir,' Dante derided. 'They tried to disinherit him, tried to change the succession rules to prevent him from inheriting my father's title, but there was no legal recourse. Tragically, his death suited them.'

Belle stroked his arm as they got into the limo, Charlie already on board, tail thumping noisily inside his plastic carrier box. 'I'm sorry.'

'As children we were never allowed a pet because my mother doesn't like animals. Tito and Carina were Cristiano's first rebellion. He used to joke that at least the presence of the dogs prevented our mother from making unannounced visits to his apartment in Florence,' he told her gruffly.

Belle smiled. 'He had a sense of humour, then.'

'In the right mood he was the life and soul of the party, but he always suffered from low self-esteem and when anything went wrong, he blamed himself.'

'Does your mother make unannounced visits to your home?' Belle asked apprehensively.

'Not for a long time. Relax… If she shows up, I will deal with her,' Dante assured her confidently.

'How far are the kennels from your house?' Belle prompted.

'A ten-minute drive.' A faint hint of colour flared over Dante's high cheekbones as he met her surprised violet eyes. 'I'll look into rehoming the dogs. It wasn't what Cristiano wanted for them but you're right, it would be kinder.'

He wasn't used to pets, having been raised without them, but her heart ached at the depth of grief and guilt that still tormented Dante. He was so very different from the man she had initially assumed him to be. His emotions ran deep and strong. There was nothing superficial about him. If she discovered that she was pregnant, she didn't believe that he would try to pressure her into doing anything she didn't want to do and that was a relief. She had had a friend once who had allowed her boyfriend to persuade her into a termination. Her friend had agreed in the belief that it would save the relationship, but it hadn't, and it had taken a very long time for her to get over the decision she had made. Belle didn't want to be put in that position, although in her case, she acknowledged unhappily, there would be no relationship to save.

The limo was travelling up a spiralling road with hairpin bends and, almost at the top of the hill, it turned into a lane. Belle was still twisting her head around to catch another glimpse of the staggeringly beautiful view of the Tuscan countryside, green hills and valleys studded with cypress trees, little pale stone hilltop villages, composed of houses with vivid terracotta roofs.

'Welcome to the Palazzo Rosario,' Dante murmured, and she swivelled back to be confronted by the magnificent mansion sited at the foot of the drive and her brows went up in stunned surprise.

'You could've mentioned that it was a Palladian palace,' she whispered in awe.

'How do you know it's the work of Palladio?' Dante enquired.

Belle flushed and her soft full mouth compressed. 'Why? Isn't a waitress supposed to know about stuff like that?' she snapped.

'Few would recognise the fact at first glimpse,' Dante told her wryly. 'I'm curious.'

'My grandfather had a great interest in architecture and a big collection of books,' Belle admitted. 'Growing up he dreamt of being an architect but, of course, it was just a dream.'

'Why?'

Belle sighed. 'When he was young, working-class boys went straight out to work as soon as they were legally able to leave school. It didn't matter how clever they were. Further education wasn't free, and it wasn't an option. Grandad worked as an accounts clerk in an office all his life.'

'But he taught you about architectural history,' Dante gathered.

'It was his personal interest. He would save up to buy these big books and then he would share the best pictures and highlights with me,' she recalled fondly, thinking once again that she had been very fortunate in her grandparents.

'I learned young as well. The *palazzo* belonged to my uncle on my mother's side, Jacopo Rozzi. He was an art historian. He never married and when he died, he left his entire estate to me, which effectively made me independent of my family,' Dante admitted. 'I owe him a great debt for his generosity.'

'Is that how you started out in business?' Belle asked curiously, climbing out of the limo to look up in wonder at the long colonnaded frontage and the perfect symmetry of the rows of tall windows.

'Jacopo invested in my business while I was still at university and got me off to a flying start.' Dante looked down at her, the glow of her usual exuberance drawing him even as he reflected in bewilderment that he had never done so much talking in his life with a woman as he had done with her. She was so natural with him and he had not had that experience with her sex before. Even the attention she was giving the *palazzo*, rather than him, was outside his normal experience and weirdly annoying.

'Belle…?' he breathed silkily before she could rush up the stone steps ahead of him, a newly released Charlie dancing at her heels.

And she turned back to him, wide violet eyes bright below the tangle of red-gold curls on her pale brow. Dark eyes dazzlingly gilded by sunlight, he stared down at her and the hunger she incited surged up inside him with volcanic force. He pulled her into his arms, one hand locking to the back of her head, his fingers meshing into her curls, and he devoured her soft, smiling mouth with his own. Taken by complete surprise, Belle stiffened and then leant into the solid heat of him, the wild, ferociously sweet taste of his hunger melting her deep down inside to create a blossoming ache of need.

Distinctly dazed by that embrace, she stumbled when he set her free and it was all the encouragement he needed to sweep her up into his arms and carry her up the steps with Charlie racing in their wake and barking to indicate his enthusiasm. Belle started to laugh. To say that they made an entrance to the *palazzo* would have been to understate the case, for a group of goggle-eyed staff awaited them there.

Belle slid down out of Dante's arms, flushed and embarrassed by his hot-headed behaviour but immediately soothed by the huge smiles that greeted their arrival. Their luggage was being brought in and she accompanied Dante upstairs. Only belatedly did it dawn on her that that seemingly spontaneous kiss had most probably been driven by Dante's desire to make them seem more like a loving couple. It had been a public statement, nothing more. At that acknowledgement, the bounce dropped straight out of her step again and she scolded herself for believing for one minute that he had simply succumbed to an overwhelming passion.

The first-floor landing was open-plan to the *piano nobile*, the main reception room according to the usual Palladian floor plan. It was certainly a very grand and richly furnished space. Indeed, her brain was already whirling with images of colourful frescoes, classic statues and more architectural detail than she could comfortably absorb in a short space of time. 'Do you use this as the main reception area?' she enquired.

'Only if I throw a party but that isn't very often. I converted rooms on the ground floor for normal life. It's a challenge because Jacopo left me a treasure house and I don't like making changes but, at the same time, I have to actually *live* here, so it has to be made fit for purpose,' he pointed out, following the luggage through a classical double doorway into a simply vast bedroom.

It was only then that Belle realised that naturally they would be sharing a room and that her nights of solo privacy were at an end, but when she laid eyes on the huge canopied bed with its incredibly opulent crimson-and-gold brocaded drapes, she burst out laughing. As if it were not imposing enough, the bed sat on a dais. 'Please tell me I don't have to sleep in that monstrosity...'

'I'll have you know that that is a genuine Louis XIV bed,' Dante informed her with amusement lighting up his lean dark features. 'And it is *very* comfortable... Look, even Charlie thinks so.'

Belle exclaimed in dismay, *'Charlie!* No!'

The terrier had searched out the most comfortable place in the room and had had no problem leaping up onto the bed and making himself at home there. She scooped him up and set him down on the floor again.

'So, you live inside a history book. I would never have guessed that about you,' she admitted truthfully.

'My parents' home is only a few miles away and I've been visiting this house since I was a little boy. I was grateful for my uncle's interest in me because I got very little attention at home,' he admitted ruefully. 'I was brought up by nannies, some better than others, and few of them lasted long because my mother is a demanding employer. Cristiano and I went to boarding school and Jacopo used to come and take us out for the day. He was a very kind man and I think he felt sorry for us.'

'Was he close to your parents?'

'No, and when he left me all his worldly goods, they were outraged because they had always assumed *they* would inherit his estate and to leave it to me, the younger, more rebellious son, was even worse in their eyes.'

'What age were you when he died?'

'Twenty-one.'

Belle shook her head, unable to even imagine inheriting the splendour of such a residence and all that went with it at such a young age. 'You have already lived a most extraordinary life, Dante, and you're not even thirty yet. You may not have been blessed in the parent department, but you were blessed in other ways,' she told him quietly.

'Do you want the official tour now or later?' Dante enquired.

'Later would be fine,' she said. 'I'm a little tired. I'd like a shower and a nap.'

'Dinner's at eight,' he told her casually.

In truth, Belle was thinking that she needed to pull back and wise up fast. She was at the Palazzo Rosario purely to play a role: that of official girlfriend. Dante had reminded her of that harsh fact when he'd kissed her and carried her in like a bride, for goodness' sake! Such a public and exaggerated display of affection would not have occurred to Dante if he hadn't been *faking* it to make them seem more like a real couple. Real couples kissed and laughed and fooled around like that, but *she* had to remember that they were *not* a real couple.

She opened a connecting door and found a bathroom, a gorgeous creation in Carrera marble with a copper bath catching the fading sunlight by the window. Dreamy, she thought, but she was too tired for a bath and would savour its delights some other time.

All her troubled thoughts were concentrated on Dante. The act of sex had plunged their arrangement into a no man's land of confusion, she acknowledged ruefully in the shower. All of a sudden she didn't know how to behave, what was acceptable, what was not. Was he expecting her to be all over him like a rash when anyone else was around? Or did the staff not really matter? Probably not, she decided, not after he had staged that big entrance for them. Now he was probably just expecting her to blend into the woodwork while he got on with his normal life. Her true moment of importance wouldn't arrive for ten days when his guests would arrive...at about the same time as she would be finding out whether or not she was pregnant.

But what were the odds? She winced. She told herself it wasn't likely but she had already calculated that that accident had happened during her most fertile phase, which wasn't good.

The door opened and she froze, telling herself off for not locking the door and ready to curl up in a heap on the shower floor. But it was Dante and he gave her a slow smile over the wall that separated the shower from the rest of the room.

'I decided that I needed a nap as well,' he husked, reaching down to pull up his T-shirt and haul it over his head, a truly spectacular network of muscles flexing to make that movement possible. Her mouth went dry and she knew that he had only been joking about the nap, her colour heightening.

She had assumed he wouldn't come near her again until they were in that big bed later that evening. She was learning that it didn't pay to make assumptions with Dante. He had told her that he was a passionate guy. He liked sex. He liked sex a lot…and he wanted her, had wanted her from the first moment he saw her, and nobody had ever wanted Belle with such immediacy or such passionate intensity. She could live in the moment, couldn't she? She watched the jeans drop, the classic V shape above his hip bones tightening as he got naked in record time. Sensation clenched low and tight in her pelvis and she was literally holding her breath, seeing Dante naked and aroused for the first time. And yes, he definitely had more than a nap in mind.

He stepped in with her, crowding her back against the tiled wall, hunger smouldering in his dark golden eyes, his body taut against her stomach, and she literally stopped breathing. A wild heat gripped her feminine core but that out-of-her-depth feeling was claiming her again. Only the night before she had still been a virgin, still shy, still ignorant of all sorts of things and, while she was no longer that naïve and unprepared, six feet two inches of Dante, naked and bronzed and wet and ready in the shower, was almost too much to handle.

Long fingers pushed up her chin so that he could see her eyes. 'Are you too tired?'

Belle trembled. 'Er…no,' she told him truthfully, barely able to catch her breath.

'Too sore?' he husked.

One of her tomato blushes gripped her from head to toe and she shook her head in urgent negative but even as she did so, she knew she was telling a partial lie. She was still tender, still very aware of what they had done only hours earlier. Yet inexplicably her body now *craved* him like a dangerous drug, as if that one act of intimacy had smashed all her defences, her inhibitions and her misgivings.

And yet, on another level, she was painfully aware that she wanted more from him than he would ever give her, and her insecurities lingered underneath. All he wanted was sex, but he wasn't feeling the magnetic mental pull, the attachment that was tugging at her, no matter how hard she tried to resist it. She was convenient, available, here only to play a role that he was *paying* her for. A role that had somehow become real, only it wasn't real because she was *not* his girlfriend and he hadn't really invited her to share his house with him. In just ten days it would all be over, and she would be gone.

What did that make of her? Did it mean she was like her mother? A woman content to be a man's plaything for a little while and gratefully scoop up the expensive treats and gifts he was prepared to provide in reward? Horror gripped her.

'What's wrong?' Dante breathed rawly, linking her arms round his neck as if she were a puppet and lifting her up against him, feeling the tension in her slender body, the little tremors running through her.

'Nothing,' she protested shakily, fighting that attack of guilty discomfiture, knowing it wasn't the same thing. Nothing that had happened between her and Dante had been planned by either of them. It had all been happenstance from start to finish.

'That kiss…outside…it set me on fire,'

Dante muttered thickly, nuzzling his unshaven cheek against her throat, his stubble abrading her softer skin. 'And the thought of you up here, getting naked in my shower was too tempting.'

'So I need to stay fully clothed at all times from now on?' she teased with a little gurgle of laughter.

'No, I'd probably turn caveman and rip them off you!' Dante growled, sucking at the skin between her neck and her shoulder to send an arrow of fiery heat darting down to between her legs.

And as he lifted his wet head, golden eyes molten with desire and framed with spiky black lashes, her arms tightened round his neck and she kissed him. There was no yesterday, today or tomorrow in that hungry kiss, no thought of any of that, no uncertainty. She simply couldn't go another moment without tasting that wide sensual mouth of his and she decided she wasn't going to beat herself up any more about what she couldn't resist. And what she couldn't resist was Dante.

With a stifled groan he braced her against the wall and then he bumped his brow against hers and sighed. 'Need a condom…rain check. Just because we had one glitch doesn't mean I should risk you again.'

'No,' she agreed as he slowly lowered her down the wall again, her body feeling hollow, plunged from the edge of anticipation to what felt like abandonment.

Dante stepped out of the shower and she heard him rifling through drawers as she finished rinsing the conditioner out of her hair, marvelling that the goop in her hair hadn't put him off. She was surprised when a pair of arms closed round her from behind and smoothed up slowly over her full breasts, fingertips lingering to pinch her nipples, reviving that hot liquid burn sensation at the heart of her.

'Had to find my wallet. I don't bring women here. You're the first,' Dante admitted.

'Where do you take them?' she heard herself ask uneasily, hurt at the thought of him with other women, telling herself off for that sensitivity, because of course he had had other women in his life.

'I go to their place...*always*,' he stressed. 'You're unique.'

But only because he hadn't had a choice where she was concerned, she reminded herself. She could hardly play the live-in girlfriend from a distance.

'Unique in every way,' Dante confided, his hands running all over her slippery body, finding the most sensitive spot, dallying there until she bucked and gasped out loud.

He spun her round and lifted her again, stunning eyes glittering like golden stars with intent as he braced her back against the wall again and sank into her with a guttural groan of satisfaction. She was caught up in the excitement, utterly abandoned to the surging sensation gripping her lower body. She needed more and then more, and he gave it to her in spades, all that she wanted until the terrible tension broke and she reached a breathtaking climax of pleasure that wrung her out.

'You see, unique,' Dante told her gruffly in

the unbroken silence that followed. 'You don't scream. You don't shout my name. You don't even tell me how fantastic that was. The irony is that I *want* you to do all those things for me.'

And she thought about that confession over dinner, all modest in a neat little dress at the beautifully set candlelit table, and the food, absolutely exquisite. She knew she would never scream for him, never shout his name, never, ever tell him how fantastic he was because the minute he got those responses from her she would be the same as her predecessors and, ten to one, he would no longer want her.

Yet the instant she caught herself having such thoughts, she panicked. Her skin turned clammy. She was thinking like a mistress, withholding on the enthusiasm front in the forlorn hope that such an attitude would help her to hang onto his interest. Her mother had been almost a professional mistress, always hooking up with well-off men, making herself indispensable until they moved her into their homes. Pleasing men had been an art form for Tracy. And Belle was determined *not* to follow in her footsteps, so there would be no scheming, no withholding, no lies. She would be straight down the middle all the way and when he ultimately rejected her, at least she would know that it was her true self he had rejected and not some false image she had put up.

CHAPTER SEVEN

DANTE STUDIED BELLE at breakfast and almost smiled.

She was half-asleep because he had kept her awake half the night. A tinge of guilt infiltrated him as he noticed the shadows below her eyes, the faint slump of her small shoulders. He was a demanding bastard and he knew it but every time he looked at her, he got hungry again. It had never been like that for Dante before. Usually after several encounters he was cooling off and on the way to the exit, but inexplicably Belle kept him coming back for more. He wasn't going to worry about it though, because in another couple of weeks even her originality would have worn off. He liked his own space, hugged his privacy and would, undoubtedly, be glad to reclaim it, which put him in mind of the room he had had prepared for her.

He brushed aside the newspapers he had yet to open. 'Belle?' he murmured. 'I want to show you something.'

Belle blinked and set down her tea, rising slowly by dint of bracing her hands on the arms of her chair. He was probably about to give her that tour of the *palazzo* he had promised, which they hadn't got around to the night before. She ached all over as if she had overdone it at the gym and she had a love bite on her neck. She had toyed with the idea of covering it up with a silky scarf and then had wondered if that uncool bruise was yet another deliberate part of his act to make them look like a more convincing couple.

Dante threw wide a door, and she stepped in and understood then. This was to be *her* room, furnished with the antiques he had bought and still a little bare, but the seat and the books and the promise of privacy were inviting. A wall of glass doors overlooked the internal courtyard, which was an ordered but highly attractive Italianate garden with box-hedged beds. Most of the plants were evergreen and the only colour of flower was white.

'This was once my uncle's office. He liked to be able to walk round the garden when he was working,' Dante told her.

And it was a beautiful room and an even more beautiful garden but it daunted her that she was only to be in his life for a couple of weeks and yet he still apparently felt the need to give her a room of her own. Strikingly, *not* her own bedroom but a room to which she could retreat when…when *what*? Maybe it was just a room she was to use as part of their couple pretence, she told herself urgently. Even so, it was hard to ignore the message he was giving her. He had to be a man who set a high value on his own privacy, had possibly even worried that she would be under his feet all the time when he was around. She would use the room as much as she could, she promised herself, flinching at the idea of being seen as an intruder, a nuisance, possibly even a *clingy* nuisance.

'This is lovely,' she said a shade uncomfortably after the thoughts she had had, and she wandered over to the armchair, smoothing an admiring hand over its soft rich upholstery. 'You never did tell me why you and the dealer were laughing about this chair...'

A slashing smile curved his wide sensual mouth, lighting up his whole darkly handsome face. 'Reputedly the chair is from a *maison close*...'

'A...what?'

'A brothel,' Dante translated gently. 'And the chair was specially designed for ladies to get into more interesting positions for their clients...'

'Oh...' Belle said, dumbfounded by the explanation, studying those swivelling arms, trying to imagine and then reddening fiercely.

'Yes...*oh*!' Dante laughed, teasing her. 'But don't worry, I'm not about to ask you to pose for me. I get quite excited enough simply seeing you in my bed...in my shower. You don't need to pose or do anything special to turn me on.'

'Just as well,' Belle fielded with a little snorting giggle as she stared at the chair in wonderment, thinking about its potential history and then laughing more heartily because she really couldn't imagine the sort of stuff that chair might have witnessed. 'Thank heaven I was born into the modern world.'

'I'll organise some more furniture and pictures for in here.'

Belle laughed. 'Don't waste your time. I'll be gone soon enough. It's not worth the upheaval it would cause. Anyway, you said you didn't like making changes to the house.'

The slam of a door and a raised female voice attracted Dante's attention to the entrance hall and he grimaced. 'I think you'd better stay in here. That sounds like my mother is paying one of her uninvited visits.'

Belle, however, was too curious about Dante's mother to take his advice and stay hidden. She moved into the doorway, listening to a female voice ranting in irate Italian and Dante's short clipped responses. She took another step forward and saw a tall woman as thin as a toothpick with ice-blonde hair. She was elegantly garbed in an ivory dress, diamonds flashing at her throat and ears, and in her gesticulating hand she held a newspaper.

'Is this she?' the blonde demanded abruptly, switching to English as she stared at Belle standing at the back of the hall. 'Don't be shy. Shy women don't latch on to men they meet in bars!'

Dante's proud dark head turned, and he extended a hand. 'Belle...'

Belle moved stiffly forward to grasp that lean brown hand and lifted her head high.

'Allow me to introduce you to my mother, Sofia Lucarelli... Belle Forrester.'

Belle didn't bother to offer her hand in greeting because the enraged distaste that made a mask of Sofia's still-lovely face was self-explanatory. She would not be receiving a welcome to Italy from Dante's mother.

'Her Excellency, *Princess* Sofia,' the blonde corrected her son thinly, and then in a dramatic gesture she flung the newspaper in her hand at Belle's feet. 'A *waitress* living in a campervan? Your uncle would turn in his grave if he knew the kind of woman you brought into this house.'

Dante's hand spread in support across Belle's rigid spine. 'No, I rather think that Jacopo would have cheered. If that's all you have to say, Mamma... I suggest you leave.'

'When I think of the women I introduced you to and you have chosen *this* creature!' she flung at him furiously before spinning on her heel and stalking back out again, heading for the red sports car parked at a slant outside.

'And the woman who just insulted *your* morals has enjoyed a hair-raising number of extra-marital affairs,' Dante told her as he walked them into an elegant drawing room. His lean, strong face was forbiddingly hard. 'My father seems to turn a blind eye. Maybe he doesn't care or maybe he plays away too. I don't know and I haven't sufficient interest in either of them to find out.'

Absorbing that admission of his mother's infidelities without comment, because she could see by the darkness of his expression that it was a sensitive topic, Belle murmured, 'You don't mention your father much.'

'My mother is the dominant partner and he supports her in everything she does. She once beat Cristiano so badly that he needed medical treatment,' he said flatly. 'My father stood by and made no attempt to intervene. That's one of my earliest memories.'

'I didn't realise there was physical abuse as well,' Belle whispered with a shudder. 'Didn't anyone ever report her? You said there were nannies.'

'Never underestimate the ability of the very rich to hide their sins and keep their secrets,' Dante said drily.

'Were *you* beaten?' she asked hesitantly.

He jerked his chin in silent confirmation.

She wanted to express sympathy, but he stood there so tall and tense that she regretted asking the question and she simply nodded and turned her head away. 'I think I'll go and have a look at some of my new books,' she muttered ruefully.

The door opened while she was down on her

knees doing exactly that and she spun round so suddenly that she lost her balance and tumbled sideways. As she righted herself with a flailing hand, Dante caught her other hand in his and pulled her upright. 'It's past time you told me something about you,' he informed her levelly. 'Or hasn't it occurred to you that, for someone as interested as you are in *my* backstory, I still know virtually nothing about you? And that's not likely to persuade anybody that we're a couple.'

Belle reddened with discomfiture and linked her hands together. 'I was brought up by my grandparents.'

'I know that. What I don't know is why,' Dante pointed out. 'What happened to your parents? Are they dead?'

'No, both are still alive…as far as I know.' Belle tensed even more and walked over towards the glass doors, half turning her back to him because she wasn't prepared to tell him *all* the facts. 'My mother was a model and she travelled a lot. That's why my grandparents took over. My parents broke up before I was born and my father didn't want the responsibility of a child,' she admitted stiffly. 'Perhaps because my mother and I spent so little time with each other, no attachment formed on her side and, once I grew up, she had no desire to stay in touch. I don't even know where she is.'

As he'd listened, Dante's lean dark features had lost their brooding tension. 'Do you *want* to know?'

'Not really,' Belle confided tightly. 'When I was a child I used to be full of anticipation if Tracy was coming to visit but her lack of interest in me hurt. You have this image, this *dream*, and the reality never even came close to the dream, so I suppose I learned to accept that that was just how she was.'

'Did you ever live with her?'

'She asked me to live with her when I was fourteen and I was so excited about it. She was living with this guy who had young kids.' Belle grimaced. 'Later I worked out that she only wanted me there to take care of the kids for her but I didn't want to face that at the time. I'd only been there a fortnight when her boyfriend made a pass at me and she saw him doing it. She packed me up and drove me back to my grandparents the same day.'

'And what happened to the boyfriend?' Dante prompted.

'She blamed me for it, not him, said I must've been flirting for him to behave like that…but they didn't last anyway,' Belle told him wryly. 'I'm sure I got the blame for that too.'

'Sounds like a charmer,' Dante commented. 'Much like my own. Not everyone is cut out to be a parent. I don't think I am either.'

Belle paled, tucking away that unwelcome admission for more private consideration. At least he was being honest about his feelings, she told herself, and she didn't want him to lie. Obviously, if she did conceive he would be an absent father, rather than a parent.

On his way back out through the door again, Dante paused. 'I'm attending an international charity benefit tomorrow evening and I'll be taking you with me. Steve and his wife, Sancha, are flying in for it. It's formal, so you may want to visit one of those salon places.'

'Do I have to?'

'Not if you don't want to… I like your hair fine as it is.' He reached out and lifted one of her hands and then the other. 'But you will have to have these done. They're all chipped.'

Belle swallowed hard and contemplated lying before deciding that that was beneath her. 'I peeled bits off to get at my nails but the extensions are glued on and not very palatable,' she admitted grudgingly.

Dante grinned wickedly down at her, relaxed for the first time since his mother's departure. 'I'll have someone come here to fix them for you. Good to know my solution is working. I haven't seen you try to nibble for at least twenty-four hours.'

'But what am I supposed to do when I'm nervous?'

'Kiss me instead,' Dante suggested lazily, tracing her full lower lip with his forefinger so that prickling sexual awareness spread through every sensitive area of her body. 'I guarantee that that will take your mind off your nails.'

But Belle backed away in haste and sat down on the brothel chair to reach for the Jane Austen she hadn't read in years. The way Dante could make her feel with the smallest touch was terrifying and a frightening reminder that she wasn't in control with him. Boundaries, there *had* to be boundaries, she told herself urgently, and she needed to impose some on herself quickly. This might not feel like casual sex because she was living in Dante's home, but it *was* casual sex and she had to stop forgetting that and coming over all warm and willing and melting every time he got close. And that was not to try to stoke his interest either, that was just to preserve her sanity and her self-esteem. Belle was determined not to be hurt when she was no longer useful to Dante and he sent her back to the UK.

Dante sent her a wary appraisal, wondering what was wrong, missing the sparkle, the teasing, the warmth she usually emanated. He strode out of the room, reminding himself that he had work piling up.

'Dante?'

He spun back to see Belle peering out at him. 'Is it all right with you if I visit your brother's dogs again?'

Dante lost his half-smile and shrugged a broad shoulder. 'My driver is there to be used. He'll take you wherever you like.'

Belle spent the rest of the morning reading and throwing a ball to exercise Charlie in the courtyard.

Dante joined her for lunch in the dining room. She spoke when he spoke but was otherwise quiet. Finally, he couldn't stand it any longer and he said drily, 'Look, I get that you're in a mood but if it's over something I've done I would rather you just told me what the problem is.'

'I'm just uncomfortable with how you're treating me,' Belle confessed.

'In what way?'

'Surely we only have to behave like a couple when we're in public? It's sort of spilling over into private times as well and *it's*…confusing.' Belle settled for the word stiffly. 'We're not in a relationship as such.'

'Aren't we? I thought we were having an affair,' Dante countered, disconcerted by her criticism and her evasive gaze. 'If we're not or you don't want that, I will back off.'

And there it was, *bang*, flung right in her face, the absolute truth that she meant nothing to him. Pale as milk, Belle nodded. 'I think that might be best for both of us.'

Dante gritted his teeth. Rejection was new to him and the shock of it hit him hard. He breathed in deep and slow. What was so confusing about an affair? But ego insisted he did not ask for further clarification. She was entitled to her space if she wanted it. Sex had never been part of their agreement. But how could she simply switch off like that? What had he done or said that had led to the change in her? Last night, she had been perfectly happy to be in his arms. But possibly he had always wanted her more than she wanted him, he told himself grimly. And possibly she wanted a peaceful night of sleep. Had he been too demanding? Too rough?

Belle shook away tears as she climbed into

an SUV to go and visit Cristiano's dogs. Well, he hadn't argued with her, hadn't tried to persuade her to change her mind, which merely proved what she had most feared: she was little more than a convenient sexual outlet on Dante's terms. And she was worth more than that, ex-waitress, formerly living in a campervan, or not, she had to set a higher value on herself.

Tito and Carina were ecstatic to see her again and she took them out to the exercise yard and began trying to teach them to sit and stay, rewarding them with treats if they got it right, but they didn't get it right very often.

'Too old and spoilt to learn,' the proprietor declared in broken English from where she was watching outside the fence.

Charlie ambled into Dante's office without being noticed and strayed into a patch of sunlight where he promptly lay down and stretched on a priceless Persian rug. When he saw him there, Dante ignored him. Charlie ignored Dante, well trained by the experience of

the restaurant, where non-dog-loving customers had also ignored him. Dante's afternoon
coffee arrived and the minute the tray arrived
on his desk and he lifted a biscuit, Charlie shot
back to life immediately to assume a surprisingly dainty begging position.

'You're clever,' Dante registered as the terrier fixed imploring eyes on the biscuit.

Rewarded with a tiny piece, Charlie gave
him a terrier grin and ambled back, satisfied,
to his patch of sunlight.

A knock sounded on the door and Belle
glanced in and saw Charlie. 'Oh, I'm sorry.
I've been looking everywhere for him. I was
going to ask you if you'd seen him.'

'He's a quiet little animal.' Dante believed in
giving honour where it was due and watched
Charlie bounce up to greet his mistress to
be lifted and hugged. 'How were the terrible
two?'

'OK. I gave them some exercise.'

'Shouldn't think they would've liked that.'

'No, they did. When they get tired they stop
being so frantic.'

Dante studied her. Her hair tumbling round her shoulders, framing the perfect oval of her face, she wore a filmy green top and cropped jeans that were complete with paw prints he doubted that she had even noticed. And she *still* took his breath away. Her pouting pink mouth, buoyant breasts and curvy bottom inspired instant lust in him and the pulsing swell of arousal at his groin filled him with angry frustration. 'Always the optimist. You like to take a positive approach to problems, don't you?'

'Usually,' she agreed.

'But not to me,' Dante derided. 'I've been judged and found wanting without a hearing.'

Belle flushed. 'I'm sorry you feel like that. I was trying to be sensible.'

'Clarify that,' Dante urged, springing up from behind his desk to move forward.

Belle winced. 'Living like this—the clothes, the jewellery, this gorgeous house—it would turn any ordinary girl's head but it's all a bit like the emperor's clothes in the fairy tale. It's not real and it's not mine and it's not going to last,' she reasoned uncomfortably, staring at him, drinking in the effect of all that devastating dark male beauty before bolstering her nerve and biting the bullet of the unlovely truth. 'And I don't want to fall in love with you and get hurt.'

A sizzling silence fell. A woman had never been that honest with Dante before and he was knocked for six by that blunt confession. 'I can't believe you said that.'

'Well, no point in lying about it, is there? After all, you can't want me getting attached to you either,' Belle quipped. 'And what you call an affair is very intense for me because I've never been in a serious relationship...and yes, I know this isn't serious for you, but for me, it *is*.'

'OK...' Dante spread expressive brown hands, taking a step back as if she had mentioned something dangerously contagious. He had even paled a little. 'But it's not love, it's infatuation because I was your first lover. You'll shake it off fast enough.'

'Er...thanks for that sage advice...' Belle

said, eyes wide as she summoned Charlie and walked out again with as much dignity as she could muster.

Dante released his breath in a hiss. He had never been in love. Cristiano had fallen for a long line of users and losers. Cristiano had been on a constant mission to find his one true love, and watching his brother had taught Dante that love was a car crash of insane hope colliding with nasty truths as the loved one revealed one flaw after another. Of course, Belle wasn't falling for him, but she had played a blinder with that argument because he wasn't about to try and touch her again. *She had frightened him off.* Quite deliberately too. For a split second he was amused but that reaction swiftly drained away.

What was wrong with him? He felt as if someone had dropped a giant rock on him. He felt weird. He needed to find another woman to focus on, he told himself fiercely, wipe out the last crazy week and forget about Belle altogether. How hard could that be? Off with the old, on with the new. That had always been his way.

Belle curled back up with her book and wondered how she would face Dante over dinner. She cringed and pressed hot hands to her even hotter face and groaned out loud. How could she have said *that* to him? How could she have humiliated herself so completely? But it was true that she was developing inappropriate feelings for him and she had to put a stop to that and the only way to stop it was to cut out the intimacy. So what if she was still stuck sharing a bed with him for show?

Belle dined alone and, after a long bath, went to bed early. Dante stalked through his usual club haunts and an exclusive party in Florence, finding something offensive about every woman who paid heed to him until it finally dawned on him that the only woman he actually wanted was, ironically, at home in his bed…and he couldn't *have* her. Was that what made her different and so much more desirable? Was it because she had rejected him? Was it his ego playing up?

Or was he more honourable than he had ever realised? He didn't want to hurt her, he acknowledged over his fifth drink. He checked into a plush city hotel for the night, not trusting himself anywhere near her in the strange introspective mood he was in. He couldn't sleep. He kept thinking about Belle in his bed and remembering how she had made him feel. Weird, she'd made him feel *weird*, he decided around dawn.

Belle woke up in an empty bed and wondered where Dante had spent the night. She felt guilty because she had clearly made him feel uncomfortable in his own home. As she went downstairs for breakfast she saw Dante mounting the steps, looking rather the worse for wear. His tie was missing, his jacket was crumpled and he was unshaven, a dark growth of stubble darkening his already-forbidding features. She bolted into the dining room at speed.

If she had had the nerve, she would have jibed, 'Walk of shame, Dante?' Only, she didn't have the nerve to confront him with a possibility that tore through *her* with the slashing pain of a knife…the very real possibility that he had spent the night with another woman.

The manicurist arrived late morning and redid Belle's nails in a dark blue that she liked much better than pastel pink. Her nails would match the long dress she had selected from her new wardrobe and she promised herself that this time she wouldn't pick at the gel finish and peel it off because she was willing to admit her hands looked much prettier. She would wear the fancy pendant and earrings he had bought and do her very best to look as though she belonged in a formal setting, even though she would be feeling incredibly nervous. She recoiled from the fear of letting Dante down in public. After all, this was what he had hired her to do: act as if they were a couple. No matter how she felt inside herself, she had to behave like his lover without being off-puttingly clingy.

Fully dressed, she went downstairs and from the top step she saw Dante pacing the big entrance hall, tailored dinner jacket shaping wide shoulders, narrow black trousers delineating long powerful legs, with the white of his dress shirt in stark contrast to the vibrant glow of his bronzed skin. Drop-dead gorgeous from head to toe but she wasn't allowed to think like that any more or look at him like that, she reminded herself doggedly.

Dante swung round to watch her descent, and something expanded inside his chest because her beauty had never been more obvious than in that stylish simple dress, her glorious hair tumbling round her shoulders just the way he liked it, a sleek split in the skirt momentarily showing a slice of pale perfect leg. And then she looked at him and her eyes didn't shine any more. He didn't remember noticing that inner glow she had had when she'd studied him but, on some level, he must have noticed because now it was definitely gone. Just as he had forecast, just as he had wished, she was moving on from him, shaking off those silly feelings she was too naïve to understand. He told himself that he was relieved, but his lean hands clenched into fists because he hadn't expected her to get over the notion of him quite so fast, and for some reason that only made his mood edgier and darker.

'Steve and Sancha are saving a table for us. At least with them present, you'll have friends around you,' Dante remarked as if he could sense her insecurities about attending an event patronised only by the wealthy.

Belle lifted her chin, tempted to say that Steve and Sancha had never been her friends, only VIP customers she had served at the res-taurant. Friendly, pleasant people, but not peo-ple she had mixed with in any social way. She said nothing, however, because she didn't want to draw attention to her nerves.

It was a social gathering way beyond Belle's experience. The benefit was being held in the splendid ballroom of a public building. Won-derful frescoes decorated the domed ceiling, the whole illuminated by giant crystal chan-deliers. And everywhere there were people: dinner-jacketed men standing in cliques, su-perbly groomed women in fabulous designer gowns and jewellery that flashed under the lights.

Dante closed his hand over hers, startling her, and began to trace a path through the crush. Steve Cranbrook stood up and waved from a table at the edge of the floor, his Spanish wife beaming at them both.

'Do they know we're faking it?' Belle whispered, stretching up to Dante's ear.

'Yes, but they're the only ones who know,' he confirmed.

Belle relaxed a little more then, knowing she didn't have to keep up an act with their companions. Sancha chattered as though her tongue had wheels, telling Belle about the international charity and the famine-relief fund. Belle asked the curvy brunette about her children, an adorable mop-headed blonde quartet she had often seen playing on the lake beach with their mother. The crowds thinned as the guests found their seats to listen to the speeches. Belle looked round the room, spotting Dante's mother, the princess, who would never let anyone forget that she was a princess, seated beside a man with greying hair, who had the same classic profile as Dante and was presumably his father.

Her attention roamed to the tables nearest theirs and then her eyes widened, something akin to a jolt lancing through her chest as she stared in astonishment at the man sitting alone at a table and staring right back at her. It was... No, it couldn't be... Could it be her father? Nine years, it had been *nine* years since she had seen Alastair Stevenson. The red hair she had inherited from him had distinguished wings of grey now, but the eyes were no less keen, his face barely lined. He would be in his late forties now, much younger than her mother and time had laid only a light hand on him.

Belle dropped her eyes, suddenly feeling sick and clammy. The father who had bluntly rejected her, who had said he wanted nothing whatsoever to do with 'Tracy's daughter' as if she were not also *his* daughter. The cruel bite of that rebuff had gone deep, and she had no doubt that he had been staring because he could barely credit that his unacknowledged, unwanted daughter could be present at a high-society charity benefit where he, of all people, had to know she did not belong. It was just one of those truly horrible coincidences, she reflected wretchedly, draining her soft drink, and what was more, after nine years, she should be mature enough to handle an accidental glimpse of the man without getting emotional.

The music started up again and as some couples took to the dance floor, Steve grabbed his wife's hand and pulled her, laughing, out of her seat.

'Excuse me,' Belle said tightly and rose from her chair.

'What's wrong? Where are you going?' Dante demanded, reacting disturbingly like a man who would prefer to keep her chained down beside him.

Belle lifted a questioning brow. 'Cloak-room…?'

The fingers closing to her wrist dropped away and he politely sprang upright, but the intense hold of the dark golden eyes below his frowning black brows continued. 'Are you all right?' he pressed, because he had never before seen her so pale that every freckle stood out in sharp relief.

'Of course, I am,' she told him through numb lips as she hurriedly walked away.

CHAPTER EIGHT

FRESHENING UP AND doing a little deep breathing to put the dizziness to flight helped to return Belle to normal.

It had been shock that made her feel ill like that, the sheer shock value of seeing her father after so many years, she reasoned ruefully as she walked back through the entrance hall to thread her passage through the knots of chattering people. And then she stopped dead, in disbelief, seeing the man she had hoped to avoid standing directly ahead of her. Dropping her head, she sidestepped in haste and then froze as a hand fell on her arm.

'Belle?' that almost forgotten deep voice prompted.

Her eyes flashed up into eyes identical to her own and she froze like a woman in front of a steep drop, fearing a fall. 'Er… Mr Stevenson?' she said stiffly.

'Do you know how many years I've been trying to track you down?' the older man asked in a pained undertone. 'How *long* I've been searching for you? And with the first words out of your mouth, you crucify me with guilt. And I deserve it. Yes, I *fully* deserve it, but I am here to ask you for a few minutes of your time. Will you give me that much?'

Belle was stunned that Alastair Stevenson had approached her, stunned by his claim to have searched for her and even more stunned by the emotional charge he was emanating, for the man she remembered had been cold and bitter and hostile.

'Please…' he added with emphasis as the silence between them stretched and stretched.

Dante was restless because Belle had been away longer than he had expected and there was something wrong. He knew in his gut that there was something wrong. Was she ill? Or had something upset her? Steve and Sancha reappeared and Steve bent down and said,

'When did Belle get friendly with Alastair Stevenson?'

That vaguely familiar name rang into Dante's inner computer chip of contacts and spat out a designation: high-flying hedge-fund manager, well known in the UK. 'Alastair Stevenson? What are you talking about?'

And Steve angled his head in the direction of the dance floor and Dante was dumbfounded to see Belle with the older man. Neither could be said to be actually dancing. They were swaying opposite each other, heads leaning forward as they tried to talk over the noise of the music, and even as Dante watched the couple with frank incredulity Alastair Stevenson reached for Belle's hand, said something in her ear and walked her off the floor.

Dante swore long and low and inventively in Italian.

'I mean, *obviously* she knows him well,' Steve pointed out helpfully. 'I've never seen him hand in hand with any woman other than his wife. Maybe he's her godfather or some relative or something.'

'I don't think so.' Dante had difficulty vocalising the words in English, but he was trying to get a grip on the rage licking at him and stay in control. 'She would've mentioned someone like that.'

'They're going outside,' Steve told him helpfully.

'They're... *What?*' Dante exclaimed, leaping upright, just in time to catch a glimpse of Belle vanishing through the French windows standing open onto the terrace to allow a flow of cooler night air.

'Does she smoke?'

'No, she bites her nails.' And if he had to make a choice Dante knew he would still pick the nails for a bad habit because it was an oddly endearing and revealing weakness. Every time her fingers drifted towards her mouth, he knew she was nervous or afraid.

Why would she go off to be alone with a married man? It didn't make sense. She wasn't that kind of woman, was she? At least he had *thought* she wasn't that kind of woman...the type to spot an opportunity and pounce on a rich man for the sake of it. Strictly speaking, she was only obligated to him for another week, he reminded himself grudgingly. He had no official claim beyond that date. Virginity at twenty-two did not indicate sainthood or fidelity or anything else, did it? He was being naïve, he, who was *never* naïve about women and the evils they were capable of.

Belle and Alastair took a table on the well-lit terrace and he signalled the waiter to order drinks.

'Just water for me, thanks,' she said awkwardly. 'So, this private investigation agency you hired to find me traced me through the newspaper photos that were published, but that was only *yesterday.*'

'And I dropped everything and ran, lest you vanish again. Wrangled a ticket for tonight, praying that Lucarelli would be bringing you with him because I didn't fancy trying to visit you at his place.' Alastair grimaced. 'I need more privacy than that to tell you what I have to tell you but I don't want to offend you by being too honest about your mother and the dreadful relationship we've had since your birth.'

'I haven't seen Tracy since my grandfather was buried and you couldn't offend me where she's concerned.'

'When Tracy fell pregnant I was young and naïve. I didn't get a legal agreement drawn up with her because I didn't want anyone to know about our fling. Instead I left myself open to paying every damn bill she sent me, and her financial demands were heavy. When I indicated that I wanted to rearrange the child support through a lawyer, she threatened to visit my wife, Emily, whom I met and married the year after I broke up with your mother. And I didn't want Emily to find out about you. I didn't want anyone to know about your existence because I felt like such a fool for letting Tracy take advantage of me,' he admitted heavily.

Belle's brows pleated. 'Why would her threatening to visit your wife worry you so much?'

'Emily's suffered from depression all her life

and she's fragile. Back then her biggest dream was to have a child, but she suffered several miscarriages and then we had a stillborn son,' Alastair revealed sadly. 'I should've told her about you *before* our marriage because afterwards I couldn't face telling her that I already had a child.'

Belle nodded slowly. 'I can appreciate you wanting to protect your wife.'

'But Emily knows about you now. Tracy can't hold that threat over me any longer and once I'd told Emily, I was free to look for you. Unfortunately, I couldn't find you. I had to *bribe* your mother even for the information of where and when she had last seen you,' he told her in disgust. 'By then I had had enquiries made and I had discovered that she had been lying to me and conning me with fake bills practically from the minute you were born. Until recently I didn't even realise that it was your grandparents who had brought you up and that you'd attended a state school with absolutely no frills and left at sixteen.'

Belle was frowning. '*Fake* bills?'

'Salaries for nannies, tuition fees for exclusive boarding schools, riding lessons, ballet lessons, private medical treatment, holidays. Everything your mother could think up she billed me for with false documents and yet you received *none* of those benefits. But I was the idiot who paid and paid and paid even in the early days when I was less affluent and it was a struggle to pay,' Alastair revealed. 'I learned to hate Tracy while she bled me for every penny she could and that was the background to my first meeting with you. I took my bitterness out on you and it was wrong and cruel and unjust. You were only a kid hoping to meet your father.'

'I got over it.' Belle sighed, lifting her hand to squeeze his arm in consolation because she was seeing a complete picture now and it changed everything she had thought she knew about her birth father. Tracy had blackmailed him and lied to him, all to scam money out of him for her own selfish use. 'Tracy *is* a bit of a money monster.'

'A bit? She left you high and dry after your

grandfather died and took off with her ill-gotten gains! Not a surprise,' her father pronounced cynically. 'But let's see if we can leave all that and her behind us where it belongs. I very much regret the way I treated you when I first met you. Can we move on from that? I would like to get to know you, and Emily feels the same way. All these years on, am I too late? Or is a relationship still a possibility?'

A wash of stinging tears burned the backs of Belle's eyes as her father reached uncertainly for her hand and squeezed it with a hopeful look on his face.

'I think we could try it, see how it goes,' Belle muttered chokily, tears shining in her eyes even as she gave him a huge smile of forgiveness. 'I know I would like that very much.'

'You chose to bring home a slut,' Princess Sofia whispered in a gloating tone in her son's ear as she brushed past him out to the terrace, where Belle could be seen, apparently so rapt by Alastair Stevenson's attention and their entwined hands that she was blind to Dante's presence only ten feet away.

Dante wanted to launch himself at the older man and beat him to a pulp with his fists. Steve was at his elbow, urging him to stay calm, seek an explanation rather than dealing out hasty words of anger and retribution. Steve was the voice of reason, but Dante was firing on pure animal instinct. Alastair Stevenson was *touching* Belle, and Dante was realising that he could not tolerate that. Being forced to witness that act of desecration was like having someone claw the flesh from his bones. And even worse, Belle was *smiling* at Stevenson, all soft and bright and trusting as she had never once smiled at Dante!

Breaking free of Steve's restraining hold, Dante strode forward, sufficient enraged heat in his condemnatory dark golden eyes to stoke a bonfire. 'What the hell's going on here?'

Alastair frowned and then abruptly rammed back his chair to stand up. 'Sorry, I've been rude keeping Belle all to myself, but I couldn't resist the opportunity to speak to my daughter again. Alastair Stevenson,' he said, stretching out a polite hand.

Anxiously having risen, her hand releasing her father's, Belle had clashed in consternation with Dante's flashing furious gaze and her entire skin surface had broken out in goose-bumps.

'Belle just…disappeared.' Dante formed the words through clenched teeth while that entirely baffling word *daughter*, bounced back and forth through his brain, cutting through the violence coursing through his bloodstream to unleash a wave of angry, confused disbelief. 'I was concerned. Dante Lucarelli.' After a perceptible hesitation he shook her father's hand.

'I was hoping that I could call and spend some time with Belle tomorrow morning before I head back to the airport,' Alastair continued pleasantly.

'Of course. You would be most welcome,' Dante responded, smoothly concealing the tempestuous emotions still rattling around inside him, the uppermost being a fierce annoyance with Belle for knowing everything about him while carefully squirrelling away her own secrets.

'I'll see you tomorrow,' Alastair told Belle with a warm smile.

Dante closed his hand round Belle's free one as she finally moved away from the older man. When her fingers flexed in his taut grip, he held on fast. Steve had melted tactfully away but his mother, to whom such diplomacy was unknown, still hovered.

'Well, aren't you a surprising little thing?' Princess Sofia commented with a cold gleam of what might have been approval in her sharp appraisal, because Belle had been upgraded in her estimation with the unveiling of her hedge-fund father.

'*Sì…very* surprising,' Dante growled in Belle's ear, his breath fanning the sensitive skin of her neck and making her flush.

'I wasn't expecting him to be here. I was shocked to see him,' Belle framed.

'Not half as shocked as I was to see you holding hands with him,' Dante bit out in a harsh undertone. 'You've been keeping secrets from me.'

'Why would you have been interested?' Belle said defensively.

'Because knowing about a father is a little more important than knowing your favourite colour or your star sign,' Dante retorted, a whip edge to that tone of dulcet derision.

Annoyance was beginning to spark inside Belle. It had been a tough evening and her emotions were all over the place. She wasn't prepared to be censured for spending twenty minutes with her father in a public place. 'But it's none of your business,' she heard herself say.

And it really *wasn't* his business, she reasoned resentfully, for Dante was merely the man who had hired her to play a masquerade for a weekend, not her husband, not her boyfriend, not anything really. She needed to keep that truth in mind and stop endowing him with an importance he neither deserved nor wanted.

Dante breathed in deep and slow to master

his temper. He could never recall being forced to work through so many different emotions in so short a space of time. There had been the concern and then the rage, the amazement and incredulity at her behaviour, followed by the anger that she could have omitted to tell him something so crucial about herself, and then a sick kind of relief he had yet to get his head around.

Some guests were already beginning to leave, and Dante seized on that excuse with alacrity, returning to their table only to say goodnight to Steve and Sancha. Stony silence fell in the limousine and Belle bridled. 'I don't know why you're so angry.'

'Don't you indeed?' Dante scoffed.

'It makes me want to thump you!' Belle told him truthfully.

'It made *me* want to thump your father. You're lucky that he identified himself before I got the chance,' Dante countered between gritted teeth.

Belle studied him in astonishment. 'And

why on earth would you have wanted to do that?'

Dante sent her a look of raw disbelief. 'You were holding his hand.'

'So?' Belle prodded with a toss of her head and raised brows of enquiry. 'What's that to you?'

And that was when Dante lost control for the first time ever with a woman. 'Because no other man should be touching what's mine!' he virtually snarled back at her.

'But I'm not yours. I'm the woman you hired to *pretend* to be yours.'

'Well, you weren't doing a very good job of it tonight, were you?' Dante raked back at her, startling her.

'I'm sorry if you feel that my behaviour embarrassed you,' Belle fibbed, because she was so annoyed with him that she wasn't one bit sorry and a band of tension was tightening round her temples, warning of the headache to come.

Dante looked heavenward in search of the cool and calm he needed, but instead the limo drew up outside the *palazzo* and Belle leapt out, smoother and even faster than Charlie in pursuit of a biscuit. Dante stalked up the front steps of his home, barely pausing in his haste to follow Belle upstairs and finally find the privacy he craved with her. Somewhere there were no listening ears, no snide remarks from his vindictive mother, somewhere he could talk to Belle and where hopefully she would return to being the Belle he was accustomed to dealing with.

'Did you tell Alastair about our arrangement?' Dante demanded.

Belle whirled round, her shoes already kicked off to soothe her sore toes and increasing the height differential between her and Dante, who was towering over her like a solid column of granite. 'No, of course I didn't!' she snapped back in wonderment that he could even ask. 'You can't seriously think I would tell my father that sort of thing…what would he think of me?'

'I don't care what he thinks of you.'

'Well, I *do.*'

'There is *nothing* sleazy about our arrangement!' Dante declared in outrage.

'I'm not sure he would agree if he knew the facts, so I'm afraid you'll have to put up with him believing that we're a *real* couple!' Belle fielded tartly.

'We might as well be. We're arguing like a real couple and I'm hoping the angry make-up sex is just round the corner,' Dante confided, watching her rounded bottom wriggle enticingly as she strove to reach the zip at the back of her neck. 'Here, allow me...'

After he had unzipped her, Belle snaked crossly out of the dress and draped it over a chair, mortified to be posing in flimsy lingerie in front of him now that that aspect of their relationship was over. 'There is *no* prospect of make-up sex,' she told him curtly.

Dante stalked forward, all silken predatory grace. His lean, darkly handsome features were taut, his high cheekbones slightly flushed. He stared down at her, stunning dark golden eyes like smouldering honey in the lamplight. 'Even though I want you more at this minute than I have ever wanted a woman in my life?'

Involuntarily, Belle faltered. '*Ever?* Seriously?'

'Seriously,' Dante intoned, framing her hectically flushed face with both hands. 'And I wanted to peel your father limb from limb because I was jealous and that was another first for me.'

And once he had explained that, all the turmoil inside her stopped churning and the oddest sense of peace enclosed her. 'Jealous?' she echoed in surprise and tickled pink by the idea. 'I didn't realise.'

'You must've been the only person in our radius that didn't realise. I almost made a complete idiot of myself assaulting your father,' Dante pointed out grittily. 'You were smiling at him.'

'Was I?' she muttered blankly, quivering as the heat of his big powerful body brushed against her lightly clad frame and his hands slid down from her face to her hips to tug her against him, the fabric tented at his groin, telegraphing his arousal as he ground against her with a low roughened moan that was compellingly sexy.

'Where were you last night?' she asked abruptly. 'Were you with a woman?'

'I got drunk and spent the night in a hotel. No woman. I wanted you but I couldn't have you,' he reminded her darkly.

What remained of her tension drained away.

'Later you're going to explain why you didn't tell me about your father.'

'Later?'

'Right now, we have much more pressing stuff on our agenda,' Dante husked as her bra drifted down to the floor and his hands swept up her ribcage to cup her full breasts, his thumbs teasing at the taut rosy buds that crowned them.

'But we aren't *supposed* to…'

'No rules any more, no boundaries.' Dante claimed her anxiously parted lips in fervent persuasion and a little moan escaped low in Belle's throat as she shivered helplessly against him. 'I can't tell you where this is going, but I can tell you that we're *not* going to stop before we've fully explored it because that would be crazy,' he reasoned thickly.

And in the back of her mind she knew he had a point because she *had* stopped them dead, believing that that was the right thing to do to protect herself. But possibly that decision of hers had come too late in the day to be of any real use and the chemistry and the feelings he ignited were still racing through her like wildfire to wreak havoc with her control. And how could she be anything but secretly flattered when Dante confessed that he had been jealous? Surely that suggested that she meant more to him than a casual lover?

He backed her down on the bed, parting her from her panties simultaneously, backing away a step to strip with an impatience and a burning brilliance in his possessive gaze that could only thrill her. She lay back watching him, wanting him so powerfully that she felt light-headed and almost drunk even though she hadn't had a single sip of alcohol. But then that was what Dante did to her, winding her up so tight with longing that she could barely function. The throbbing ache of need between her thighs was unbearable.

He came down to her, naked and bronzed and hot against her cooler skin, swiftly discovering that she was in such a state of anticipation before he even began to touch her that foreplay was unnecessary. He took the invitation and plunged into her hard and fast and deep. Her whole spine arched as the pleasure rolled over her in a wild, wanton surge. She couldn't fight the hunger and she no longer wanted to. The lusty ferocity of his strong body over and in hers electrified her with breathless excitement. Her heart hammered, the mesmerising rise of pleasure expanding relentlessly as the pace picked up. She soared to new heights, her body clenching tight before the rippling aftershocks of convulsive delight seized her.

Dante slumped down. 'Was I too rough?' he groaned, running his mouth lightly across her peacefully closed lips.

'No, I liked it.'

'Was I fantastic?' he murmured raggedly.

'Nope, sorry, you're never going to get that word out of me,' she told him roundly.

'But I did make you scream,' Dante responded with an unholy grin of satisfaction.

Belle had been too far gone to know what she was doing, so she let him have his moment of glory. Dante leapt out of bed and lifted the house phone, speaking briefly before scooping her up to take her into the shower with him.

'Time to tell me about your father and why you gave me the impression that he wasn't part of your life,' he chided.

'Because he never has been and I only met him once before tonight,' Belle admitted.

'Once?'

'Tracy was always very cagey about giving me any details about him. His name was on my birth certificate though. She told my grandparents that he was a deadbeat dad. She visited us when I was thirteen and she was in a real rage about Alastair refusing to pay for something and accidentally dropped a few details about where he worked,' Belle divulged.

'I faked being sick at school so that I could get out and I caught the train into London to track him down. I was curious...' Her voice died away, her face shuttering.

'Of course you were. *And?*'

'I'll explain *his* side of the story, which I only got tonight, because I don't want you thinking too badly of him,' Belle continued and, while she washed her hair, she told him about her mother's greedy con tricks and threats and her father's marriage.

'I get that he would be hostile after she put him through all that,' Dante conceded grimly. 'But how did he treat you when you first met him?'

'He seemed to think that I was there looking for money from him, which I couldn't understand because I didn't know then that the money Tracy gave my grandparents came from him and, of course, she was only giving them a tiny part of it. He said he didn't want a daughter, that I was a...a mistake who had cost him a fortune and that he had no interest in having a relationship with me,' Belle told him shakily as Dante urged her back to the bedroom where the late supper he had ordered for them already awaited them.

'You were a thirteen-year-old,' Dante remarked curtly. 'That was inexcusable.'

'I was devastated.' Belle shook her head in troubled recollection, her eyes hollow. 'I'd worked out by then that my mother had no natural affection for me, but for my father to be even colder and reject me completely was even worse.'

'I'm beginning to wish I had punched him hard,' Dante confessed grittily. 'I don't care how rough a time he had dealing with your mother. You were still his daughter and once he had first-hand knowledge of what a horror your mother was, he should've been checking up on your welfare, *not* putting his wife first, *not* keeping you a dirty secret, *not* blaming you for your mother's greed.'

'What does it matter? It's all water under the bridge now,' Belle reasoned ruefully. 'I'm willing to give him a chance. I don't have *any* other family, Dante…'

'And if you can give *me* a second chance,' Dante contended reluctantly, 'I can scarcely argue about you giving him one as well. At least he's finally got around to telling his wife about you.'

'Yes, that was a relief,' Belle agreed sleepily, setting down her empty cup and snuggling into him.

She was a snuggler. That was not Dante's style.

He let her sleep before peeling her out of her towelling robe and setting her back below the sheets on her own side of the bed. Ten minutes later she was back snuggling against him and he heaved a sigh, finally and grudgingly acknowledging that he had begun to slide superfast into a relationship of the kind he had always avoided and that he still didn't know how that had happened.

On the other hand, he had Belle back in his bed and wasn't that enough? It was the best sex he had ever had, and clearly, it had brought out a possessive, jealous streak in him that he also hadn't known he had. She wouldn't want him to tell her that, but it was the truth, he reflected as he took stock. He liked her, which was more than he could say for most of his former lovers. She made him laugh. He was even learning to tolerate Charlie, currently stretched out and dead to the world below the bed.

But he didn't do love and he was never going to do love and yet love, he sensed, was what she would want from him. Did she even grasp that love wasn't something he could pull out of a hat and flourish like a white rabbit? He didn't have that capacity any more. That ability had died in him. He had loved his parents when he was very young. He had loved nannies who'd departed without even saying goodbye. And with the single exception of his brother, Cristiano, he had taught himself not to become emotionally invested in anything or anybody because loving always, *always* led to betrayal or bitter disillusionment.

The following morning, Belle awaited her father's arrival, full of nervous tension.

'So, what do I say to him if he asks about us?' she pressed Dante uncertainly over the breakfast table. 'I mean, he's almost certain to ask. How do I describe us? What do I tell him?'

Black hair gleaming in the sunshine, Dante gave one of his fatalistic shrugs, a flawless fluid movement. 'There isn't a label, a definitive word. Whirlwind romance? Casual? That you'll be back in London and easily able to see more of him soon enough?' he suggested lazily.

Belle dropped her attention to the pristine tablecloth, her complexion slowly turning the same shade of white. Her stomach lurched with nausea. In a handful of words, he had crushed her expectations and she felt as though he had removed an entire layer of skin from her shrinking body. *Casual?* Even after he had said that they would be exploring where their relationship took them? Evidently, it wasn't going to take them very far.

He saw her returning to London, exiting *his* home and *his* life much faster than she had naïvely envisaged. He saw no sort of a future for them. She had seriously misinterpreted his words the night before, had read into them so much more than he intended. Her heart sank.

CHAPTER NINE

DANTE PACED THE elegant waiting room like a caged tiger while Belle averted her attention from him. It didn't help that he looked hauntingly beautiful, even in a blue shirt and jeans, smooth and sleek and sexy enough to attract the eye of every woman they came into contact with, from passers-by on the street to the receptionist who greeted them, to the nurse who dealt with them.

She was praying that the test would come back negative and that she would not be pregnant. When her life felt as though it was on the edge of falling apart, what else could she hope for? Certainly, she didn't feel she had the right to *want* to be carrying Dante's child when he so obviously didn't want her to be.

Her period was only two days late, she reminded herself, but she knew the basic symptoms of pregnancy and her breasts were unusually tender and swollen. She linked her hands tightly together on her lap, wishing that Dante would quell his apprehension and sit down.

A week had passed since her father had visited her at the *palazzo*. Father and daughter had got on very well, but Alastair Stevenson had admitted his concern that she was living in an uncommitted relationship. His questions had made it impossible to avoid telling him the truth. He had also agreed that she was an adult and that it was really none of his business, but it had been obvious that his conviction that she was likely to be hurt had overcome his tact. He had said nothing to her, however, that Belle had not already said to herself.

Belle was painfully aware that when it came to Dante, she had been naïve, impulsive and far too keen to believe what she wanted to believe. Over the past seven days, however, she had coped simply by ignoring the situation. Dante had made his intentions clear and she had to handle that as best she could. It was ironic that he had been incredibly considerate and attentive since he had demolished the ground beneath her feet. Of course, he was probably practising the couple pretence for his guests, Eddie and Krystal, due to arrive that very evening for dinner. Belle was dreading their arrival because she would have to monitor her every word and action in their presence.

The nurse returned with a smile to show them back in to see the English-speaking doctor Dante had sought out to do the pregnancy test. Belle swallowed hard as she took her seat.

'Congratulations,' the middle-aged doctor told them with a beaming smile.

Belle dared not look in Dante's direction and was disconcerted when he reached for the fingers she had raised to her lips and kept her hand in his. For the remainder of the appointment she felt as though she were trapped inside a bubble, detached from the real world. It was shock, she knew that because, even though she had had her suspicions, confirmation and being told the date that she could expect to give birth hit her with the force of a sledgehammer.

'That was interesting,' Dante commented, tucking her back into the powerful sports car he had driven her out in.

Belle blinked, baffled by that as a first comment.

'At least we can still have sex,' Dante added, plunging her deeper into confusion.

'But I won't be here for you to have sex with,' Belle said waspishly. 'I'll be back in London.'

'That's not going to work,' Dante intoned flatly.

Seriously? His first reaction to her accidental pregnancy was 'We can still have sex'?

Dante shot a glance at Belle's pale, stiff profile. She hadn't even giggled, and she usually had a terrific sense of humour. But then she had shown all the animation of a zombie from the moment the doctor had congratulated them. She might as well have been told that she had only six weeks left to live. Maybe she really, *really* didn't like children, he reflected, wishing he had raised that thorny subject instead of carefully avoiding potential obstacles throughout the week. Maybe she was simply appalled at the prospect of motherhood and the changes it would bring.

Dante had spent the entire appointment worrying about Belle's weird response to the news that they would be parents in a few months. He hadn't had the time or space to be shocked on his own behalf. It had crossed his mind that his own parents would be triumphant at the continuation of their precious family line, but that was merely an irritant. Dante had swiftly moved on from regretting the vasectomy he had never had and the promises he had once made to himself in the heat of youthful rebellion and an understandable desire for revenge. He was twenty-eight years old, way past the stage of needing to spite his unpleasant parents to score empty points. After all, nothing could bring Cristiano back and nothing could change his parents into decent people.

How *did* he feel about the news they had received? he asked himself. Apprehensive about the challenges that lay ahead, he acknowledged, for nothing in his own childhood had taught him how a decent father should behave. But he could learn and, in the short term, there was a tiny spark of excitement growing inside him because Belle was carrying his baby. Not only did that increase his possessive attitude towards her, it was also sending images of what their child might look like crashing through his brain. Shock was doing that to him, he reasoned.

'I think that we should leave this whole matter on a back burner until *after* our guests have departed on Sunday,' Dante breathed tautly. 'It's an emotive subject and we don't want to get into it now.'

Belle stared out fixedly at the beautiful Tuscan countryside as the opulent car crested another hill and swept down the other side, that swooping sensation making her tummy lurch with nausea. He didn't even want to *talk* about the baby. Or was it simply that he didn't want to risk her getting upset before Eddie and Krystal arrived? And why his use of that word *emotive*? Dear heaven, was he planning to ask her to consider a termination? She broke out in a cold sweat.

At least we can still have sex. Was there any mood in which Dante did not want to have sex? The past week was a blur for Belle of being intercepted in the midst of whatever activity she was engaged in and lured away to the nearest dark corner/bed/sofa/shower. Once even in the garden, where she had been playing with Charlie.

Saw you out here... Couldn't resist, cara mia, Dante had groaned hungrily, his hands hard on her hips as he made her rise and fall over him until the world went white and she lost the power of speech.

Dante was insatiable and, admittedly, she couldn't resist him either, but she *had* attempted to give him some space and take a sensible step back from that incessant intimacy. In fact, she had spent a lot of time curled up reading in 'her' room but had soon learned that it wasn't *her* room at all because Dante was always striding in to demand to know what she was doing, even though it was obvious. He would tell her that she shouldn't read depressing books, drag her off on a drive or out to lunch in Florence and once even to meet his 'friend' Liliana, for coffee. Liliana, who wasn't a friend at all! Liliana, a gorgeous brunette barrister, had studied Belle with indignant, envious eyes and had barely spoken to her, saving all her attention for Dante, who had not even seemed to notice the tense atmosphere between the two women.

And then there were the gifts, unsought, unwelcome, even the tiny solid gold replica of Charlie on a chain. There was the cashmere shawl he had purchased one morning when he was convinced she was cold because she had shivered with awareness while he stroked her spine with an abstracted hand and she was too embarrassed to tell him the truth. There was the handbag she had paused to admire in a shop window before she had learned that, with Dante in tow, to look at anything for sale was synonymous with saying, 'Buy it for me, please.' He was generous, far too generous, a good trait for a man to have.

Sadly, however, none of that meant that he was ready to support her in having his child. If she had his child, she and that child would be in his life for years and years and he probably didn't want that, but if she was to choose a termination, his life would return to normal and she would leave it again. That would be that, she conceded sickly. It would sever their connection for good and wasn't that what Dante *always* wanted from a woman?

The freedom to walk away? Wasn't that why he had hired her in the first place?

As a stranger, you'll walk away afterwards without a problem. You won't cling or believe that I have any further obligation towards you, nor will you assume that having helped me out makes you special to me in any way.

A baby was an obligation, a lifelong obligation, one he wouldn't want, she reasoned unhappily, any more than her father had wanted it when he had been a younger man.

'I've got something I have to say to you,'

Belle murmured tightly. 'I won't consider a termination.'

'I wasn't planning to ask you to consider that option,' Dante retorted in crisp dismissal. 'That's not on the table.'

'Oh…' Drained by the removal of that pressure from her mind, Belle sagged, suddenly tired but able to think about the baby she was carrying without frightened conflicted responses getting in the way.

Her baby, her little family, she savoured without guilt. It didn't matter that her child hadn't been planned, not the way she had always hoped, it only mattered that her child would be healthy and that she would manage to be a more loving, caring mother than her own had been.

'Where are you going?' Dante enquired as she went upstairs once they had arrived back at the *palazzo*.

'I feel like a nap,' she admitted self-consciously. 'I can't afford to be falling asleep on your guests this evening.'

'*Our* guests,' Dante corrected.

'Yes, I must try to stay in role,' she conceded ruefully.

The happy live-in girlfriend, confident in her position in Dante's life and newly in love, everything Belle *wasn't* feeling just at that moment. She wondered how Dante was feeling and then remembered that that wasn't to be discussed until the weekend was over.

Dante got stuck into work, refusing to dwell further on what they had learned. It had happened. He would deal with it. That was how Dante dealt with challenges. He didn't emote, he didn't rage and he didn't whinge. He would process the development and decide on the best way forward.

Eddie Shriner was a heavily built man in his forties with brown hair and keen grey eyes. Krystal was a tiny blue-eyed blonde with voluptuous curves shown off by a fitted skirt and a low-necked top. She had the low, husky voice of a seductress. Even Belle had to admit that the blonde was a classic beauty but the knowledge that Dante had bedded the other woman made her uncomfortable.

Krystal, however, wasn't the least bit uncomfortable to find herself in the company of her husband and a former lover. Krystal's calculating blue eyes locked onto Dante like a heat-seeking missile the instant she walked through the door and she virtually blanked Belle when she was introduced to her, choosing not to comment on the fact that both women were English born and bred.

Dinner was challenging with Krystal's nonstop attempts to grab Dante's attention with flirtatious comments, which repeatedly interrupted the men's conversation. Krystal liked, possibly even expected, to be the centre of male attention, Belle registered, and seemed to have little time for other women. Krystal pretty much ignored Belle's presence at the table and resisted her efforts to engage her in conversation.

When a member of staff moved to fill Belle's wine glass, Belle covered it and asked for water instead.

Krystal stared and lifted a questioning brow. 'You don't drink?'

'No,' Belle confirmed, because even before she had realised she could be pregnant, she had not been much of a drinker. Alcohol gave her an out-of-control sensation that she didn't enjoy.

'Ah…a problem drinker,' Krystal assumed snidely. 'That must make socialising difficult for you.'

'Actually…' Belle breathed, bristling with the urge to empty a glass of water over Krystal's purring head. Krystal was so smug now, convinced she had identified Belle's fatal flaw and keen to drag it out into the open to humiliate her. A fierce desire to lay an even more basic claim to Dante assailed Belle. 'I'm not drinking because Dante and I are expecting our first child…'

At that spontaneous announcement, Dante's arrogant dark head whipped round in their direction fast, dark golden eyes glittering in the candlelight, his jawline clenching even as Eddie offered them his warmest good wishes.

Indeed, Eddie, who was not entirely blind to his wife's penchant for Dante, beamed at the news and relaxed back into his seat.

Krystal, on the other hand, went rigid, her blue eyes locking like knives to Belle, her shapely mouth compressing into a tight line. 'My goodness, that's quick,' she commented. 'From what I understand, you've only been together for a few weeks.'

'Sometimes,' Dante inserted with a glance at Belle's heightened colour, 'that's all it takes.'

'Yes, I knew Krystal was the woman for me the day I met her,' Eddie chipped in cheerfully.

'You should've kept the baby a secret,' Dante censured when Belle emerged from the bathroom later that night.

Clad in the pyjamas she had stubbornly retained and continued to wear, Belle ignored the sexier garments provided as nightwear with her new wardrobe. Even for Dante, Belle refused to dress up like a mistress or behave like one. To her way of thinking, a mistress strove to attract and retain her lover's interest in her body and used that same body to cement her hold on him. And she wasn't prepared to do that.

'You should have told me the baby *was* a secret,' Belle replied with spirit, but, in her heart of hearts, she knew she had blurted out their secret because Krystal had made her jealous and she had wanted to strike back.

'I wasn't expecting you to make an announcement,' Dante imparted.

'A baby definitely makes us look like more of a couple,' Belle argued, engaged in combing her wet hair to tease out a knot. 'Krystal was surprised and furious.'

'And now she'll target you rather than me.'

'Isn't that better? The more attention she gives you, the less her husband likes it,' Belle pointed out, having carefully watched the interplay round the dining table.

'I'm not sure you can cope with her bitchiness,' Dante breathed, snatching the comb out of her fingers with a curse word in Italian. 'Stop that! Let me do it. The way you're doing it, you won't have any hair left by tomorrow!'

Belle stood still while he calmly teased out the copper tangle and tossed the comb down on the dresser again. 'Thanks. I've met a lot of sharp-tongued women in my time, Dante. I'm not a pushover. I can handle anything she throws at me.'

'Fortunately, we'll be busy tomorrow flying out to see the land and you shouldn't be exposed to her that much,' Dante commented.

'I'm tough. This is, after all, what you *hired* me to do,' Belle reminded him tartly.

Dante grimaced. 'I can do without that reminder now,' he told her tautly, stepping back from her to walk over to a table and tear a sheet from the pad there. 'I want to get what I owe you out of the way now. Write down your bank details and I'll organise the payment straight away… OK?'

No, it wasn't OK. Hugely taken aback, Belle stared down at the blank sheet. Her cheeks burned, her mouth quivered, and her eyes were full of pain and mortification. He was *still* determined to pay her, and she didn't want it now, didn't want that reminder of how they had met and what they had agreed to, because nothing had happened the way it was supposed to happen.

'I don't want the money any more, of course. I don't,' Belle confessed wretchedly, looking up. 'It's like you're paying me for sex.'

'I've never paid for sex, so why would you twist everything up and accuse me of that?' Dante demanded angrily, colour flaring over his high cheekbones.

'That's what it *feels* like to me!' Belle argued, refusing to be silenced.

'I pay my debts and I *owe* you it,' Dante framed harshly. 'Let's not make it an issue.'

He sent her a brooding appraisal as she sank down on the end of the bed, his dark eyes aglow with censure, his lean, darkly beautiful face grim with restraint. 'We have enough to worry about without arguing about trivialities.'

Obviously, he meant the baby, she reflected painfully, the baby that he saw as a problem and she saw as a blessing. She supposed she would put the money away for the baby since he was determined to pay it and she printed out her bank details with a heavy heart. He strode out of the room and eventually she slid into bed, too tired to agonise any more and reluctant to greet Krystal over breakfast with the visible evidence of a troubled night. Her phone beeped and her head lifted again because she didn't receive many texts, her friends in London having gradually fallen out of touch when she'd failed to return from France.

With a sigh she scrambled up again and lifted her phone, frowning when she saw an unfamiliar number and then stiffening when she saw the message. It was Tracy, her mother, who had had her number for over three years and hadn't once used it, nor had she ever replied to the occasional text Belle had sent.

Belle's soft mouth tightened, and dismay filled her when she read Tracy's message. Tracy was in Italy and wanted to meet up with her for a catch-up. Belle frowned, unable to imagine anything they would have to catch up on and wondering how the older woman had even found out that her daughter was in

Italy as well. Her frown deepened. After what she had learned from her father, she wanted nothing more to do with her mother, but she shrank from meeting up with her just to tell her that. She texted back an apology and said she was just too busy before getting back into bed, troubled by unpleasant memories of her long-absent parent.

While she was trying to sleep Dante was standing in his office with knotted fists. Once again, he had screwed up with Belle because he hadn't foreseen her reaction. Women were so sensitive, or, at least, Belle was, reading stuff into gestures that wouldn't even have occurred to him. He had wanted her to have the money, so that she knew she did not need to feel trapped. He hadn't *wanted* to give her that choice, but he had known he *should*. He didn't think she would wish to rely on her father for financial help. That relationship was still too new and their past history regarding her mother's greed too delicate. He wondered how on earth he had ended up with a woman who treated his wealth as though it were something toxic. She was way too keen to turn her back on everything he gave her, determined to ask for and accept nothing. It did not bode well for the future.

Belle woke up in the morning in an empty bed, a slight dent in the pillow next to hers the only evidence that Dante had joined her late and risen before her. Disturbed that he had kept his distance throughout the night, which would surely give him a new record for restraint, she wondered if the discovery that she was pregnant was already encouraging him to step back from her.

She went down to breakfast, garbed in the prettiest dress she could find in her wardrobe because Krystal was one of those ultrafeminine women who made every female in her radius feel overshadowed. She had expected to see Dante already at the table out on the shaded loggia overlooking the magnificent view of the valley below but the only face that greeted her was Krystal's.

'I think I threw the staff into a panic when I

came down, but I've always been a very early riser,' Krystal remarked in the friendliest tone Belle had yet heard from her.

The blonde watched as Belle was served with tea and reached for a croissant. 'I gather you're not suffering from morning sickness.'

'Probably not far enough along yet for that and then maybe I won't get it. The doctor told me that not everyone does,' Belle responded lightly.

'Are you hoping that Dante will ask you to marry him?' Krystal asked baldly.

'No, my mind doesn't work that way. I'm very independent,' Belle fielded smoothly.

'That's fortunate, with Dante being so anti-marriage. He's a total commitment-phobe, which is why I moved on,' Krystal declared with a little shudder of her slight shoulders, implying that her relationship with him had been of a longer duration than it had been. 'Of course, with his history, what can you expect? His brother was badgered practically from birth to marry and produce an heir for the family, and now that he's gone, Dante's expected to take on the responsibility…and he's always sworn that he will *never* marry or have a child.'

'Yes,' Belle agreed quietly as if nothing the blonde had told her was news to her. But she was faking it because she hadn't made that connection between Dante's background, his brother's passing and Dante's strong aversion to commitment or having a child. No, she hadn't put it together for herself even though she had had almost all the facts. After his childhood, the very last thing he would want to do was fulfil his parents' fondest wish and continue the family gene pool. Luckily for Belle, however, she had not once dreamt of Dante proposing marriage and had not even considered that unlikely event.

'But couples don't marry these days simply because there's a child on the way,' Belle pointed out, amused when Krystal's eyes hardened at her lack of reaction.

Dante appeared then with Eddie. Apparently, Eddie had wanted a tour of the *palazzo* and the estate. A helicopter awaited their trip, and as Dante lifted her into the craft, Belle had cause to regret a choice of clothing that was impractical. Before very long, however, she had something more pressing to worry about. While Eddie was enthusing over the hundreds of unspoilt Tuscan acres he had bought up and urging the two women to properly appreciate the spectacular views, Belle was discovering that the motion of the helicopter made her feel queasy and she was finding it a struggle not to be sick.

Her legs wobbly, Belle got out of the helicopter and merely sought the nearest cover to conceal her weakness. She darted behind a concealing tree and was horribly sick. A supportive hand tugged her hair out of the way and stroked her back.

'You turned green while we were in the air. I knew you were ill,' Dante admitted. 'But I thought it better not to mention it...'

Her head swimming, Belle leant back against his lean, powerful body for momentary support. 'How's the deal coming along?'

she whispered, desperate to take his mind off what she had just done.

'Eddie wants to sell the whole lot to me, not only Cristiano's piece. I've agreed,' Dante said succinctly. 'I'll turn the majority of it into a nature reserve, but I'll keep my brother's woods private.'

'It's a lovely way to remember him,' Belle murmured softly.

'On the way back we're being dropped off at the cabin. I want you to see it,' Dante told her. 'We can drive home from there, so you won't have to fly again.'

And there he was once more, being considerate when she least expected it, Belle thought painfully, resting her clammy brow against his shirt front, fighting to muster the courage to detach herself from him when she so badly wanted to cling. She breathed in the rich familiar scent of cologne and husky male and the combination made her head swim with longing. Of course, Dante would be in a good mood with Eddie having agreed to sell the land to him. He had got what he wanted out of their arrangement even if he hadn't got what he wanted when it came to Belle. There was no way Dante *could* want their unplanned child. He had always been honest with her but now he would feel forced to prevaricate, for he could hardly admit the truth.

And she hadn't admitted her own truths either, had she? Belle scolded herself as she joined their guests to admire the fabulous landscape from the hilltop. She tried to pinpoint the exact moment when she had fallen headlong in love with Dante. It had begun in Paris, long before she had even seen that her heart was at risk; it had begun when he opened up and told her about his brother and his family. Slowly but surely, she had begun to see that, much like her, Dante had not received the love he'd needed as a child and, because of that, he shied away from any hint of that emotion, automatically distrusting it.

Belle's grandparents had loved her, but as she'd grown up she had felt increasingly guilty that her mother's lack of interest had meant that her grandparents were forced to raise a child in their retirement years. Dante had only known his sibling's love and, without being shown love, it was hard to trust enough to *feel* love. Yet for Belle, the more she had learned about Dante, the more she had loved him. It had been a slippery slope she'd raced naïvely down at dangerous speed, intimacy making her feel deceptively close to him when she wasn't because he didn't return her feelings.

Krystal and Eddie flew on to Florence for lunch while Dante and Belle were deposited in a forest glade overlooking a small tranquil lake. A two-storey wooden structure met Belle's curious gaze. 'It's very modern,' she commented.

'When Cristiano first had it built it didn't have electric or heating. He liked to come here to unwind after a demanding week at the bank. I talked him round and my company installed the windmill and the turbine in the stream and the solar panels.' As Belle gazed around the tall woodland trees and savoured the tranquillity, she said, 'Wasn't it rude of us to leave Eddie and Krystal behind?'

'No. Krystal said she'd seen enough countryside to last her a lifetime and Eddie wants to take her shopping to put her in a better mood,' Dante retorted, unlocking the cabin door. 'It's not very large…'

Belle wandered into the cosy interior, surprised to see a picnic basket and a chilled bottle of wine awaiting them on the table near the stone hearth. 'Who are these for? Where did they come from?'

'The staff brought over food for our lunch. You have to eat,' Dante reminded her. 'Inside or outside?'

'Outside,' she said, glancing round the cabin, recognising that there was little to see but the walls and the furniture because it had been stripped of any personal possessions. 'Anywhere there's shade.'

Dante spread the rug. Belle removed her shoes and sank down cross-legged to investigate the contents of the basket and lift out plates. Breaking open a soft drink, she murmured, 'It's a beautiful place. Did you come here a lot to see Cristiano?'

'Often,' Dante said gruffly, poised between her and the sun, a lean, powerful figure with a shock of black hair and the golden eyes of a tiger. 'He used to sleep outside on the roof during the summer and he made a point of not using the electric I had installed for him. He preferred lanterns. He was at peace here...at his best.'

'The dogs must've loved it too,' Belle mused, wondering why he had yet to sit down and why his lean, darkly handsome features were so tense.

'We have to have a serious discussion,' Dante informed her tautly.

'I thought we were waiting until Eddie and Krystal were gone.'

'Last night I realised it couldn't wait any longer,' Dante incised. 'We have a child to plan for *now*.'

'*I'll* deal with the baby stuff,' Belle parried firmly, nudging the filled plate she had prepared for him in his direction. 'Aren't you hungry?'

'Not really.'

An uneasy little silence fell.

'It's my child too.' Dante, it seemed, was still set on making his point. 'Naturally I want to be fully involved.'

Belle frowned. *'Do you?'* she asked, her incredulity unhidden.

Dante crouched down lithely on a level with her, black denim stretching taut across his muscular thighs, and a current of hunger rippled through Belle, which she tried to suppress. 'A child doesn't have to be planned to be wanted,' he murmured with assurance. 'I want to *marry* you, Belle...'

'No, you don't,' Belle told him with complete confidence, even as her heart squeezed tight with stress and heartfelt regret that that should be the case. 'I know the gossip columnists went mad over you moving me into the *palazzo* with you only *because* you're famous for being a commitment-phobe. A man with that outlook is unlikely to welcome a child into his carefree life, because there is no bigger or more lasting responsibility than a child. Please don't tell me polite untruths to impress me.'

His stunning eyes shimmered, his wide, sensual mouth compressing. 'I'm not trying to impress you. Everything changed when you came into my life—'

'Yes, I screwed it up,' Belle broke in sharply, steeling herself against his arguments. As she saw it, she was protecting them both from the possibility of making a terrible mistake. Marrying a man who only wanted to marry her because he thought he had to and who didn't love her would be a disaster. 'I fell pregnant. You feel responsible.'

A raw glitter lit his eyes. 'I do *not*.'

'You feel so responsible you're willing to go against your own nature and offer a solution you have never wanted,' Belle condemned tightly, anxiety and pain licking cruelly at her because she considered a proposal made out of pity and the conviction that she couldn't cope alone truly humiliating. 'But I am perfectly capable of returning to the UK and making my own life and bringing up my child.'

'Of course, you are, but that's not what's best for either of us. I want to be with you. I want to be with my child,' Dante bit out impatiently, angry that the dialogue was going even worse than he had expected. He hadn't expected enthusiasm, nor had he expected the level of resistance she was giving him.

'You should know me well enough to know that I would never try to keep you away from our child and that I will happily agree any reasonable access arrangements,' Belle protested.

'That's not enough.' Dante vaulted back upright, poured himself a glass of chilled wine and leant back against the cabin to study her. 'I won't give up on this, you know. I'm very stubborn when you challenge me.'

Belle breathed in deep and slow. Her eyes were prickling and stinging with the tears she was holding back. She blinked hard and angled her attention away from him into the trees. She couldn't bear to marry him because she was pregnant, couldn't bear to reach that position in his life and then watch as whatever physical attraction she held for him slowly waned until finally they had nothing left but their child to share. He deserved better than to have to marry a woman he didn't love, and she deserved better than a man who didn't love her.

'You've until tomorrow evening to think over my proposal,' Dante breathed tautly. 'I have a funeral to attend in Brittany tomorrow. I'll be leaving in the morning.'

'The employee who died?'

'Such a waste of a good man.' Dante sighed. 'There were other positions he could have gone for. He didn't need to work at heights.'

And that was why she loved Dante. He genuinely cared about his employees. Even though that workforce ran into quadruple digits, he sincerely regretted the loss of one. He had a heart even though he didn't acknowledge it. That was why she had to withstand his innate desire to do 'the right thing'. He felt he had to marry her because she was pregnant and that was an outdated idea, and unnecessary.

She would manage fine on her own. It would make her much unhappier to marry him and then lose him again.

Krystal and Eddie departed early the next morning and Dante left not long after them, a new distance in his attitude to her. He was annoyed with her for refusing to marry him, she conceded ruefully, because he had decided that *that* was the magical solution to the baby he saw as a problem. But a marriage wouldn't solve the baby complication, it would only create more problems.

Belle went to visit Cristiano's dogs that afternoon and arrived back at the *palazzo* to be informed that she had a visitor waiting for her.

Consternation gripped her when she walked into the elegant drawing room and saw Tracy comfortably ensconced in an armchair, flicking through a fashion magazine over a cup of tea.

'Well, you've certainly landed on your feet here,' her mother mocked as she cast down the magazine and stood up, a tall slim blonde in her fifties, who looked a good decade younger than her years.

CHAPTER TEN

'RELAX,' TRACY URGED as Belle parted her lips. 'I was discreet. I didn't identify myself as your mother, only as a friend. I'm quite sure you've glossed over your downmarket background with Dante. It's never wise to remind a man that you come from a lower level of society than he does.'

Belle relocated her tongue. 'What on earth are you doing here?'

Tracy raised a brow, her green eyes hard. 'It's your own fault. You said you were too busy to see me. What did you expect me to do?'

'Take the hint and leave me alone,' Belle said ruefully. 'As I did three years ago when you left me in London broke and dossing on someone's couch.'

'You're still my daughter.'

'The daughter you never wanted,' Belle reminded her. 'And yet you used me to con thousands and thousands of pounds out of my father, which you certainly never chose to share with Grandad and Gran, who were raising me for you.'

'So, you've seen Alastair and listened to his lies?' Tracy assumed angrily. 'And you *believe* them?'

'Yes, I'm afraid I do,' Belle admitted tautly. 'I've got nothing more to say to you and I can't imagine what you're doing here.'

'You're not that stupid,' Tracy told her. 'Naturally I'm here hoping that you will share a little of the pot of gold you're living in.'

'I haven't got any money to share,' Belle retorted sharply.

'He must give you an allowance, at the very least…'

'No, he's terribly stingy,' Belle told her without skipping a beat.

'I wonder how stingy he would be if I threatened to approach the press and sell the whole *sordid* story of your background…and believe me, there are dirty details you know nothing about,' Tracy told her with a sneer.

Belle had paled but she stood her ground. 'I shouldn't think Dante would give a damn,' she countered. 'I definitely don't think he would let you blackmail either of us.'

Tracy swept up her clutch bag with a flourish. 'If you change your mind, you have my number. We'll see…won't we?'

Belle didn't breathe again until her mother drove off in the taxi she had had waiting for her outside. She felt quite sick and dizzy from the stress of Tracy's visit and her shoulders hunched as she registered that her mother had asked her not one single question about her well-being or her relationship with Dante. Tracy simply saw her as a potentially profitable source she was keen to milk. Of course, that was all she had ever been to her mother, the cash cow she used to punish Alastair Stevenson for not marrying her. She blinked back tears of hurt and hated herself for that weakness because it was a long time since she'd had any illusions about Tracy.

But there was no denying that she was horrified at the idea of Tracy approaching the tabloid press with some cooked-up and no doubt sleazy story to sell about her. That would embarrass Dante, and Belle couldn't bear the concept of that because Tracy was her cross to bear, *not* his. In fact, the only way she could protect Dante from her mother was by leaving him because, if she was no longer living with him, nobody would be the slightest bit interested in buying a story about her ordinary self. Dante, after all, was her sole claim to fame.

Perhaps Tracy had done her a favour by jolting her out of her comfortable groove in Dante's opulent home. Belle knew that she didn't belong under Dante's roof. Now her job was done. Eddie had agreed to sell Cristiano's land back and Dante was paying her for her two weeks in his life, paying her handsomely too. That would provide her with a nest egg for their baby.

She needed to leave Dante. Of course, she would get in touch again in a few months, by which time things would have settled down and he would have accepted that marriage hadn't been a very good idea. What was the point in her staying? If she went, he would have his freedom back. Staying, she decided wretchedly, would be clingy, considering that he had never once asked her to stay on and had already paid her for pretending to be his girlfriend.

Furthermore, if she stepped away now, she would hopefully begin to get over him. If she stayed, however, she would probably surrender and end up marrying him while falling deeper and deeper in love with him. Being only briefly his wife and becoming accustomed to the joy of having a proper place in his life and then having to leave that security would ultimately hurt her much more. A short-term shock of severance would be easier for her to bear than getting involved in a marriage destined to die when Dante's interest faded.

But getting back to the UK with Charlie in tow quickly was impossible, for there were all sorts of regulations to be met. Travelling back to France, on the other hand, would be relatively easy and cheap. She would travel by train and return to the campervan until she got Charlie's travel documents sorted out. She didn't have much to pack because none of the new clothes would fit in a few months and, obviously, she wasn't taking the jewellery with her. But maybe she should take it to sell at a later date for the baby? Dante would pay child support, wouldn't he? He wouldn't abandon them, she told herself urgently. He would be relieved, though, when his most pressing problem moved out from under his roof.

Tears tripping her, Belle packed a small case, gulping and swallowing back the thickness in her throat and the increasingly terrifying image of having to live without Dante. He'd only been in her life for two short weeks and he had turned it upside down. He had walked into her heart and taken up residence there and she couldn't imagine her life without him, which probably meant that she was one of those stage-five clingers he had mentioned and despised.

She had managed for years on her own and

she would manage again. Two weeks were two weeks and hopefully she could return to the level-headed, practical being she had been before he'd got a hold of her. That belief taking charge, she opened up the laptop Dante had given her for her use to research train schedules.

Dante returned to be informed that Belle had left earlier that evening with Charlie and a suitcase.

It took him a moment or two to process that information. She couldn't have walked out on him, he told himself, because no woman walked out on Dante. He had always been the one to do the ditching and the walking away. Now it seemed it was his turn to see the other side of the fence. There was a note in the bedroom, the jewellery he had bought her stacked neatly beside it, so the breezy, 'Thanks for the money, I'll be in touch' note didn't really have the effect she might have hoped.

Belle had refused to entertain even the thought of marrying him. He had known from

early on in their relationship that she didn't
have a mercenary bone in her tiny curvy body
So, it wasn't a question of her having gratefully taken the money and run. He didn't credit
that. Yes, she had been upset by the marriage
proposal, but not enough to leave him over it.
If he had been in the mood to laugh, he would
have savoured the reality that asking Belle
to become his wife had upset her rather than
pleased her. He, who had long known himself
to be one of the biggest prizes on the marriage
market and the target of every designing single woman, had been shot down in flames.
But, sadly, he wasn't in the mood to laugh
there in that empty bedroom without Belle.

He hadn't got halfway to the funeral he
had attended before he had realised where he
had gone wrong with the proposal. He hadn't
said a tenth of what he should've said. He had
struck out because he had put his pride first.
He hadn't told her he loved her. He had been
too proud to put that out upfront. He swore
under his breath and attempted to picture his
life without Belle. So bleak was the picture he

summoned up, he paled. She had even taken the dog with her!

He strode downstairs, all business now that he knew what he had to do. He checked the laptop he had given her, scrolled through her past history and smiled at the ease of discovering her travel plans. She had gone back to France. Why France instead of the UK, he had no idea, but he was enormously grateful for that stroke of luck because he believed he knew where she had gone and he could get there faster than she could to await her arrival.

Late afternoon the following day, Belle staggered out of her taxi outside the restaurant and paid the driver. She was worried about how she was going to eat for the next few days because Dante's payment had not yet reached her account and the long journey had cost her more than she had expected. She released Charlie from his travel carrier and he went bonkers at having his freedom back, tearing around and then letting out a startled bark and changing direction to go pelting down to the beach. Setting the box and her case to one side, Belle stared to see who had attracted Charlie, and then she noticed the tall dark man poised below the pine trees. The terrier leapt and jumped around him in joyous greeting.

Belle knew only one man who her dog greeted with such enthusiasm. Dante might pay Charlie very little attention, but Charlie was, inexplicably, devoted to Dante. But it couldn't *be* Dante, she reasoned, her heart thumping very fast as she walked down to the beach, her shoes crunching in the sand, getting closer and closer. The man moved out of the dappled light into the sunshine and she stopped breathing altogether, disbelieving the evidence of her own eyes. His luxuriant blue-black hair blew back from his bronzed and beautiful face and her throat closed over as he moved towards her.

'Standing here again takes you back two weeks, doesn't it?' Dante intoned. 'We didn't know each other then. We didn't know what was ahead of us.'

'How the heck did you know where I was?' she gasped.

'Looked at your browsing history on the laptop. You should've brought it with you, although I am very glad you didn't because I would've wasted time trying to track you back to England. Why did you come here?'

'I have to make arrangements for Charlie and I don't have the money yet,' Belle admitted, turning red.

'So, only if I keep you as poor as a church mouse can I hang onto you?'

'You don't want to hang onto me.'

'What am I doing here then?'

'Making this split harder on both of us,' Belle told him heavily.

'But I don't *want* to let you go. I have absolutely no intention of letting you go and would go to any extreme, no matter how ridiculous, to *keep* you,' Dante intoned with fierce determination. 'I won't insist that you marry me but I *will* keep on asking… I'm being frank about my ultimate goal.'

Belle shook her head dizzily. 'What the heck are you talking about?'

'You're looking a touch green again,' Dante noted, urging her over to the concrete bench below the trees. 'Sit down. Take a deep breath, and while you're doing that, *listen* to me.'

As she sat, Dante dropped down into a crouch in front of her and reached for her hand. Stunning dark golden eyes intercepted hers. 'I want to marry you because I love you and making that commitment is important to me, but if you can't face the wedding ring, you can still live with me until the day you die. Nothing less is acceptable...'

Wide-eyed, Belle stared back at him, her colour fluctuating. 'How on earth are you in love with me?' she mumbled.

'Your guess is probably as good as mine. I don't know how it happened, but it did happen very fast,' Dante mused reflectively, his lean, strong face serious as he quirked a black brow in self-mockery. 'One day I was planning to live alone for the rest of my days and the next I'd changed out of all recognition. I wanted you with me. I wanted you with me *all* the time. When you weren't immediately in front of me, I had to find you and know what you were doing, which is why you never really got to enjoy that room of yours for very long on your own. You entered my life and became an incredibly precious part of it.'

'P-precious?' she stammered.

'Very,' Dante confirmed, lifting her fingers to his mouth and kissing them and then checking the nails. 'You've been peeling again.'

'Yes…when I'm stressed, I slip,' she said thickly, wondering if she could dare to believe what he was telling her, if it was actually possible for a man like Dante to fall in love with someone ordinary like her. 'But what if you're imagining that you're in love with me?'

'Why would I do that when I didn't want to fall in love in the first place?'

'Maybe…because I'm pregnant?' she suggested uncomfortably.

'Yes, that *did* increase your desirability once I got over the surprise of it,' Dante admitted. 'But I was already in love with you and fighting all these emotions I never allowed myself to feel before—'

'You kept on reminding me that I would be going home to the UK,' Belle protested.

'As I said, I was fighting what I was feeling and in denial, but I wouldn't have gone as far as actually *letting* you leave me,' Dante assured her confidently. 'I was kind of lonely before you came into my life. I've always been rather solitary in my habits, but you pull me in, take me out of myself, make me happy. Before you, only Cristiano could achieve that feat. So, obviously I'm going to fight to the last ditch to keep you. You're mine. I know a good thing when I find it and I'm not letting you go.'

'Oh, Dante...' Belle whispered. 'Walking away cut me in two but I thought it was what we both needed, although if Krystal hadn't reminded me how anti-marriage you were and my mother hadn't shown up...'

His brows pleated. 'Your *mother*?'

'Tracy, yes... Yesterday, she was after money,' Belle confided in discomfiture. 'I don't know how she found out I was with you.'

'A friend called to tell me that a photo of us together appeared in an English tabloid.'

'Well, Tracy threatened to go and sell some story about me to the newspapers and would probably make up lies to make it sleazy.'

'She threatened you and tried to blackmail you? That is exactly what she did to your father!' Dante interrupted angrily. 'But you don't deal with her, you don't need to. That's my job now. But she can sell whatever stories she wants to the newspapers, it doesn't bother me. If she tells any lies about you, however, she will find herself dealing with the full weight of the law because I *will* sue.'

'But what will your family think about that kind of stuff?'

'Do you think I care? The truth of what went on in my childhood home behind closed doors is more sordid than anything that could be pinned to you,' Dante derided. 'Don't forget that I grew up with my mother's constant affairs with other men and her abuse and that soured my view of women from an early age. The casual affairs I indulged in didn't improve that view…but then, to be fair, I *chose* women who were content to settle for sex and a good time with a rich man. And then I met you and you taught me that there was another kind of woman out there, one who could be warm and trustworthy and caring and who didn't care about my money.'

Tears glimmered in Belle's violet eyes. 'That's quite an accolade. Are you sure you're not seeing me through rose-tinted glasses?'

Dante laughed. 'No, definitely not. You are much too fond of homeless animals. You bite your nails and you are also very untidy and disorganised.'

'I'm not…and I've stopped biting them!'

'You *are*. I keep on tripping over the shoes you leave lying around,' Dante told her without hesitation. 'So, I think we needn't worry about me seeing you through rose-tinted glasses.'

'It's all right to retain a touch of a rose tint,' Belle told him in reproach as he tugged her upright. 'I'm sure I've loads more faults than you've noticed yet, but I do love you an awful lot.'

'And yet you ran away from me!' Dante lamented. '*And* you refused to marry me—'

'I honestly did believe that you didn't *ever* want to get married or have a child.'

'I did think that way until I met you but much of my resistance to those concepts was driven by a powerful need to disappoint and punish my parents for what they did to my brother and me,' Dante admitted wryly. 'But, with you, I *want* a wife and a family, and yes, it's unfortunate that that news will delight my mother but I'm not about to sacrifice my happiness to punish her.'

'Perhaps in time you'll mend fences,' Belle suggested uncertainly.

'Never. I wouldn't trust my mother near our child either. She doesn't like children. No, it will always be safer to keep my parents at arm's length,' he told her firmly.

'So, when did you decide that you wanted to marry me?'

'The minute I recognised that my home felt like a home for the first time because *you* were in it,' Dante admitted, lowering his handsome dark head to hungrily claim her readily parted lips. He kissed her breathless and her hands closed into his shirt front and then slid up to grip his shoulders, happiness finally daring to take her in a stormy surge as she allowed herself to believe that he loved her.

'You're really not worried about what Tracy might do?' she pressed. 'You see, that's partly why I left. I wanted to protect you from her.'

Dante smoothed gentle fingers through her tumbled hair. 'I'm not worried about Tracy. I can handle her and it's my job to protect you, not the other way round,' he asserted.

'Why did you insist on paying me that money?' she whispered. 'That was very off-putting.'

'I didn't see it in that light. The money was yours and I wanted you to have it. I didn't want you to feel trapped in my home because you were pregnant and financially dependent on me. I wanted you to feel that you had choices because you've *never* had proper choices,' Dante explained feelingly. 'But I wouldn't have parted with a penny had I known you would leave me.'

'How do you really feel about the baby?' Belle asked.

'Excited…but please, no twins, not until I at least learn the ropes of being a decent parent.' Dante sighed. 'Fortunately, we'll be learning together and we both know what to avoid from our own childhood experiences.'

'Yes, we know what not to do,' she agreed, noticing how dark it was becoming and frowning. 'Dante, where are we going to spend the night? I don't think the campervan will meet your standards.'

'What standards?'

'There are probably reigning monarchs in the world today who don't sleep in as fancy a bed as you do,' Belle told him squarely.

'I wasn't planning on us retiring to the campervan,' Dante said gently. 'I phoned Steve. They have a very acceptable poolhouse guest suite prepared for us and I'm expecting to have to suffer through a great hail of I-told-you-so when I introduce you as my bride-to-be, because he was always telling me that there was a woman out there somewhere for me. Oh, that reminds me…'

Dante was digging into the pocket of his tight jeans and pulling something out. He lifted her left hand and pushed a ring onto her ring finger without ceremony.

Taken aback, Belle studied the glittering ring on her finger, a fancily cut sapphire surrounded by diamonds. 'I still haven't said yes to marrying you,' she reminded him.

'You want me to get down on bended knee or something?' Dante asked bluntly.

'No, I want you to promise to tell me that you love me every day and I promise to tell you the same thing,' Belle murmured with a huge smile.

'Done. I love you so much more than I ever thought I could love anyone, *cara mia*. I thought I had an icicle for a heart and you took a blowtorch to the ice,' Dante murmured raggedly. 'Now that we're in a serious relationship, does it mean I can drag you under the trees and have my wicked way with you to celebrate that I've finally got you?'

'Nope. I'm not arriving at their chateau with my hair standing on end and covered in sand.

I also want the comfort of the pool house. I'm turning into a material girl,' Belle warned teasingly as she bundled up Charlie and they walked to the campervan parked behind the restaurant, picking up her case on the way.

'*My* material girl,' Dante breathed possessively, casting her an appreciative appraisal. 'My woman, soon to be my wife, and I couldn't be happier.'

Belle stretched up to kiss him before climbing into the campervan. 'So, do you think Cristiano's dogs could come home to us now?'

'Yes, I've been resigned to that idea for at least a week and having competition will keep Charlie on his toes, but they are not *all* welcome to sleep in our bedroom,' Dante informed her firmly.

Belle massaged the long muscular thigh flexing beneath her fingers.

'Then again, if your persuasive tactics are daring enough to impress, I'll think it over,' Dante admitted, on fire with pure lust.

EPILOGUE

DANTE WALKED ONE step through the front
doors of the *palazzo* and was engulfed, literally, by dogs, kids and an armful of fragrant
wife.

'You didn't say you'd get back early,' Belle
exclaimed, thrilled that he was home for lunch
on Christmas Eve.

'I like to surprise you,' Dante admitted.

'He's lying,' Steve Cranbrook piped up cheerfully from the doorway of the drawing room.
'He gets antsy when he's away from you too
long. Five years married and he's still trying
to play it cool. Where do you get the energy
from, Dante?'

'I'm high on life,' Dante murmured, curv-
ing Belle under one arm, scanning the splen-
didly decorated hall and the big Christmas
tree she had ornamented with such care and

enthusiasm. In the space of five years, Belle had turned his life inside out and upside down and he loved it.

But their children were the biggest revelation. Luciano had come along first, red-haired and dark eyed, followed by Cristiano, dark of hair and eye, and then little Violet, the chubby toddler sucking her thumb while hanging onto his leg to stay upright, with her mother's hair and eyes and so laid-back in comparison to her brothers' rampant energy that she was almost horizontal. Dante had never expected to enjoy his children as much as he did while he watched their different personalities and temperaments emerge as they developed. And they were each one different, a smorgasbord of their parents and their genes, and he loved them all.

Tito and Carina, greying with age, wriggled as he moved past in greeting. These days they didn't get much livelier than that and hugged their beds in a huddle. Even Charlie had slowed down a little, although the addition of a mate and then a litter of puppies, none of whom Belle initially wished to part with, had led to Dante declaring a moratorium on breeding. They had four dogs, but it was a constant battle to keep the number down with Belle having taken an interest in a local animal rescue society and seeing all too many needy causes. The courtyard rejoiced in two tortoises and the children had rescue rabbits and guinea pigs. The *palazzo* was overrun with animals.

'Dad and Emily will be with us by teatime. They got held up in London,' Belle told him as they mounted the stairs, the hubbub of Steve and Sancha's children and their own squealing with excitement as they played tag falling away behind them.

'I need a shower.' Dante sighed. 'But first…'

'First,' Belle repeated, gazing up at him as if he hung the moon, an expression on her face that he never ever got tired of seeing because he knew he wasn't worthy of it, knew he couldn't possibly deserve the amount of happiness she had brought into his life.

'Shower,' he framed doggedly, knowing that

if he touched her, he wouldn't stop because he had been without her for four days, and four days was a very long time for a man like Dante to go without his very sexy, very beautiful wife.

Belle breathed her husband in like the addict she was. 'You smell gorgeous... The shower can wait, and you look so sexy with stubble.'

And that was it, Dante was all out of fight, backing her down on the bed and claiming her passionately and thoroughly to sate a need that never quite quit. '*Dio...* I love you so much, *cara mia*. I can't get enough of you.'

He vaulted off the bed, naked and bronzed, to grab his jacket and brought out a box. 'Early Christmas present,' he explained, flipping it open to reveal a diamond bracelet that shone like a river of fire across his darker skin.

Belle lay there in a sated huddle, trying to summon up the energy to return to their guests and the million and one things she had to supervise as a wife, a mother and a hostess. The diamonds glittered round her slender wrist and a smile slashed Dante's darkly beautiful features because he loved to see her wearing the stuff he bought her. 'I need a diamond chain to lock you to the bed and then I wouldn't have to share you with anybody.'

Belle lay back, revelling in being quite ridiculously happy, thinking that having lived through all the lonely, stressful times had been worth it when she looked at her current contented life with Dante.

Her father and his wife, Emily, had slowly become part of the family, grandparents to their growing brood of children. Emily was kind and lovable and she adored kids. Belle was much closer to Emily than she had ever been to her mother or even her late gran. Dante had had one meeting with Tracy to warn her off and Tracy had never bothered them again. Belle had got to know her father bit by bit, visiting him and his wife in London when Dante was in the UK for business. In return the older couple had visited Italy and had been waiting at the hospital when Luciano was born, sharing in their joy at the birth of their first child. They had shown the same interest when Cristiano and Violet were born, and Belle truly valued their enthusiastic approach to being grandparents.

Steve and Sancha were equally close to them, looking after their children when, occasionally, Dante and Belle wanted some alone time as a couple and sharing most family holidays with them. For their last wedding anniversary Dante and Belle had spent a glorious week rediscovering each other on a Greek island. Cristiano's log cabin had been extended and in the summer they frequently slept on the roof under the stars, although Dante only did so as long as he had every comfort on the market with him. In the woods, they got back to nature, fishing and exploring and the children and their friends' children absolutely loved those carefree weekends.

As for Dante's mother, they occasionally ran into her at public events and exchanged polite nods of acknowledgement. Dante's father had passed away two years earlier after a severe stroke. Princess Sofia sent magnificent gifts every time her son had another child and had once dared to drop in and seek the reassurance that her grandchildren were being taught their proud history. But although Dante had become a prince on his father's death, he refused to use the title, deeming that snobbish superiority that had tainted his parents and persuaded them to have children they didn't want too dangerous to nurture in his own family.

'We're going to have another wonderful Christmas,' Belle told Dante cheerfully as she emerged from the shower. 'All the family and friends round the table together, healthy and happy.'

'I was never a people person. You're the one who made that miracle possible for me,' Dante told her, appreciative eyes resting on her as she raced around the room getting dressed.

'We *both* did,' she contradicted softly. 'You had to let love in before our life could happen—'

'I didn't so much let love in as get run over by the equivalent of a ten-ton truck!' Dante teased her. 'Meeting you changed my life.'

Belle grabbed his hand, stretched up to kiss

his freshly shaven cheek and gave a little wriggle of sheer appreciation as she looked up at him with her heart in her eyes. 'I love you *so* much…'

'Not half as much as I love you,' Dante told her confidently.

* * * * *